BLOOM WHERE YOU ARE

The Companion Workbook to the Award-Winning

BLOOMING IN BROKEN PLACES

DEBORAH MALONE

LAMP POST
publishers

OTHER BOOKS BY DEBORAH MALONE

Blooming in Broken Places

Trixie Montgomery Cozy Mysteries
Death in Dahlonega
Murder in Marietta
Terror on Tybee Island
Chilled in Chattanooga

Skye Southerland Cozy Mystery Series
Buckhead Dead
Decatur Dead

BLOOM WHERE YOU ARE
by Deborah Malone

Published by:

LAMP POST
publishers
SPRING VALLEY • CALIFORNIA
www.lamppostpublishers.com

ISBN-13 # 978-1-60039-242-9

Acknowledgments

Over the years there have been many people who have helped me on my writing journey. Some gave me encouragement, some advice, and some just a pat on the back. All of these people, too numerous to name, have been instrumental in keeping me writing. If you are in this special group then I thank you from the bottom of my heart!

Contents

BLOOM
WHERE
YOU ARE

CHAPTER ONE

MIRIAM

DAY ONE

No! It's Mine and You Can't Have It!

Then Jesus said, "Come to me, all of you who are weary and carry heavy burdens, and I will give you rest. Take my yoke upon you. Let me teach you, because I am humble and gentle at heart, and you will find rest for your souls. For my yoke is easy to bear, and the burden I give you is light."

Matthew 11:28-30

Because I'd grown up caring for Mother, who suffered with Rheumatoid Arthritis, I'd developed a false sense of responsibility for everyone and everything. When I was just a kid, my little cousin, Ronnie, had come over to visit. He wandered off on his own and it took a while before we found him.

Well, let me tell you, I gave him a lecture he has probably never forgotten. I let him know right away that I was responsible for his safety, and he shouldn't have gone off without letting me know. Of course, he wasn't my responsibility, but in my mind, I had been with him, and he was in my care and I let everyone down by not watching him.

Miriam had a huge responsibility when she was a child. Her mother, Jochebed, had asked Miriam to watch out and make sure her little brother Moses would be safe while hidden in the reeds. Not only did she stay with him until the Egyptian princess found Moses, she was brave enough to tell the princess she knew of a lady that could nurse him. Jochebed was allowed two more years with Moses until he was weaned.

During the Exodus, God gave Miriam the responsibility of leading the women on their journey to the promised land. God, also, appointed her a prophetess, which means she was a messenger of God's word.

Even though God had given her a great task Miriam wasn't satisfied. She turned to Aaron, their brother, and complained to him that God had given Moses the most important of jobs. It really doesn't come as a surprise that Miriam, big sister and protector of Moses, couldn't understand why he had more authority than she did. After all, she was his big sister and protected him when he was a child.

...But the Lord heard them. So immediately the Lord called to Moses, Aaron, and Miriam and said, "Go out to the Tabernacle, all three of you!" So, the three of them went to the Tabernacle.

Numbers 12:2,4

To me this was the equivalent of Dad saying, "Deborah Jean, come here right now!" I knew when he used both of my names I was in big trouble. God called Moses, Aaron and Miriam to his side into the Tabernacle so they would remember who's ultimately responsible. Have you ever felt the need to not only do your task, but take on others as well? I think we've all done that at some time or another. But God doesn't want us on overload. We need to let others help us as well as give some of the burden to God. After all, he has told us, "For my yoke is easy to bear, and my burden is light."

"So don't worry about tomorrow, for tomorrow will bring its own worries. Today's trouble is enough for today."

Matthew 6:34

Application Questions:

What responsibility are you taking on that isn't yours at all? For example, are you trying to change someone or tell them what to do?

_____

_____

_____

_____

_____

_____

_____

DAY TWO

Why Me Lord?

Look after each other so that none of you fails to receive the grace of God. Watch out that no poisonous root of bitterness grows up to trouble you, corrupting many.

Hebrews 12:15

As kids we used to play in the woods behind our house. Sometimes we'd run through a burr patch and come home covered with burrs. A burr is a prickly husk on a seed that has teeth. As you walk by, they hitch a ride on your clothes or in your hair. There were times after running and playing in the woods I'd come home covered with these sticky hitch hikers.

As a caregiver, I experienced many emotions that became sticky hitchhikers. Anger was a big one. Anger that my mother was sick and I had so much responsibility at a young age. Anger that my daughter Niki was sick and I didn't understand why. There isn't a person who hasn't dealt with anger – even Jesus experienced anger while on earth.

In the temple area he saw merchants selling cattle, sheep, and doves for sacrifices; he also saw dealers at tables exchanging foreign money. Jesus made a whip from some ropes and chased them all out of the Temple. He drove out the sheep, scattered the money changers' coins over the floor, and turned over their tables.

John 2:14-15

Unwelcome memories flood my being when I think of this emotion. After my daughter Niki was diagnosed with a brain tumor, I became angry with the world. I guess you could say I was having one humdinger of a pity party.

I am so thankful for my friend, Vicki, who taught me it's all right to laugh and have fun even during the sticky times. She showed me by doing. We'd take our daughters, throw their wheelchairs on top of her old station wagon, and take off to the mountains. There were times we laughed so hard we lost our breath – and it felt good! This didn't take away the sticky burrs, but it sure made getting rid of them easier.

God doesn't say we shouldn't get angry, but to resolve it quickly. "*...Don't let the sun go down while you are still angry, for anger gives a foothold to the devil*" (Ephesians 4:26).

The longer the burrs were left entangled in my heart the harder it was to get them out. Removing them quickly was easier than letting them stay where they didn't belong.

Have you ever experienced the anger burr? Whether you're a caregiver of an active toddler, sick and/or disabled child, spouse, or parent, you will pick up the anger burr – it is inevitable. Over time, I discovered asking for help doesn't equal a sign of weakness or failure as a caregiver. It is a necessity!

But God didn't leave us alone to try and untangle the burrs that are unreachable. The Bible tells us in Psalm 46, "*God is our refuge and strength, always ready to help in times of trouble*" (Psalm 46:1).

Application Questions:

Do you ever ask God, "Why me?" When you're going through a hard time, ask him instead, "What would you have me learn?" Do this so you won't get covered with sticky burrs like anger and self-pity!

_____

_____

_____

_____

_____

_____

_____

_____

DAY THREE

Beam Me Up Scotty, I'm Drowning!

When I am overwhelmed, you alone know the way I should turn...

Psalm 142:3

Have you ever had the urge to climb under the bed, hide in the back of the closet, or maybe sit on the basement steps? Anything to get away from the responsibility that sucks the life right out of you. My hand is raised. There have been many times in my life I felt like I was literally drowning. I couldn't get my breath. That's when the urge to disappear would rear its ugly head.

As an example of the responsibility I shouldered as a young child, every day as I arrived home from school, I wondered would Mother be at home or in the hospital. I've felt the urge to hide from it many times. I would dare say most people have.

Ask Moses. Sometimes we must do things that aren't comfortable. God appeared to Moses in the burning bush, giving him the grave responsibility of going before Pharaoh demanding the release of God's people. You would have thought, growing up around the Pharaoh, he wouldn't be afraid.

> *Then the Lord became angry with Moses. "All right," he said. "What about your brother, Aaron the Levite? I know he speaks well. And look! He is on his way to meet you now. He will be delighted to see you. Talk to him and put the words in his mouth. I will be with both of you as you speak, and I will instruct you both in what to do. Aaron will be your spokesman to the people."*
>
> *Exodus 4:14-16*

This conversation between God and Moses validates feeling overwhelmed at times is normal. Even though God was frustrated, okay angry, he did not leave Moses to bear the burden alone. Does God leave us alone today to bear our responsibilities? Have there been times that you've felt alone when you've had to shoulder responsibilities?

Let's look at what the Bible has to say.

Then Jesus said, "Come to me, all of you who are weary and carry heavy burdens, and I will give you rest. Take my yoke upon you. Let me teach you, because I am humble and gentle at heart, and you will find rest for your souls. For my yoke is easy to bear, and the burden I give you is light."

Matthew 11:28-30

When you feel overwhelmed, accept Jesus' invitation to help you carry your burdens. What a blessing that he is always there for us!

Application Questions:

What makes you feel overwhelmed? Do you remember to yoke yourself to Jesus when you feel that way?

_____

_____

_____

_____

_____

_____

_____

_____

_____

DAY FOUR

Let It Go! Let It Go! Let It Go!

I pray that your hearts will be flooded with light so that you can understand the confident hope he has given to those he called – his holy people who are his rich and glorious inheritance. I also pray that you will understand the incredible greatness of God's power for us who believe him...

Ephesians 1:18-19

Just like Elsa in the movie *Frozen,* sometimes it would be better to let it go. If it were just that easy. "It" could pertain to several hindrances in our lives keeping us from being our best selves. For example, we might need to let go of relationships, fear, sin, guilt, past mistakes, slander, anger, bitterness, failures, regrets, worry and a bushel-full of other feelings that could come between us and our Abba.

Something else that can come between us and God is basing our identity on what we do.

When I was growing up, Mother had Rheumatoid Arthritis and was on crutches by the time I was able to understand she needed help with almost all of her daily activities. Being the only girl in our family I was thrown into early adulthood helping Mother run the household. But the responsibilities didn't stop there. Not long before Mother died, my youngest daughter, Niki, was diagnosed with a brain tumor at the age of three. After the surgery, she contracted Meningitis which left her severely disabled.

Being so involved with the daily care of others, I never realized just how much being a caregiver influenced how I thought of myself. I didn't know how much until Niki transitioned into a personal care home. I can't tell you how many times I wished I had just one day where I didn't have to worry about another's needs, but after Niki moved into her new home, I experienced a feeling I never expected – being lost.

I'd been a caregiver most of my life, and now I felt as if I'd lost my identity. We tend to get our self-worth from what we do and not who we are. It's hard to let go of that role. When Niki transitioned into her new home, I held onto the role of caregiver like a tick on a hound dog.

I guess you could say I wasn't going to give up the role of responsibility easily. I eventually realized who I was did not depend on what I was doing. I had to let go of all the old to make room for a relationship with Abba. Someone once said, "Let go of the past so God can open the door to the future."

Have you been so busy as a caregiver that you have let that role take the place of your role as the precious child of God that you are? Remind yourself of your true identity in Christ. Let go of basing your identity on what you do; instead, base it on *whose* you are, and see what God has in store for you.

> *"For I know the plans I have for you," says the Lord. "They are plans for good and not for disaster, to give you a future and a hope."*
>
> Jeremiah 29:11

Application Question:

Do you base your identity on what you do or whose you are?

_____

_____

_____

_____

_____

_____

_____

_____

_____

DAY FIVE

Miriam

Anger, fear, guilt, anxiety. Have you ever felt any of these emotions when you feel overwhelmed with the responsibility of everyday life? Which one do you identify with?

_____

_____

_____

_____

_____

_____

_____

Miriam was thrown into responsibility at a young age. Responsibility was no stranger to Miriam. God chose her to be a prophetess - a messenger of God - and she was also a strong leader of the women. When they crossed the Red Sea, she led the women in song.

Then Miriam the prophet, Aaron's sister, took a tambourine and led all the women as they played their tambourines and danced. And Miriam sang this song; "Sing to the Lord, for he has triumphed gloriously; he has hurled both horse and rider into the sea."

Exodus 15:20-21

According to Exodus 15:20-21 what jobs did Miriam have during the Exodus?

_____

_____

_____

_____

_____

_____

_____

Wow, Miriam, must have been absolutely perfect for God to use her in such a way. Miriam had accomplished much in her life. She'd shown how heroic she was while watching out for baby Moses. Not only by protecting him, but she had the ability to think quickly enough to ask the princess if she needed someone to nurse him. She had shown strong leadership to the other women in the wilderness and great faith in God.

This proves that God uses only perfect women, right? Well, not exactly. Because you see this isn't the end of Miriam's story. Even though Miriam chose to please God, she fell short. She and Aaron had important positions, as we have discussed. Miriam was a great leader of the women – but she and Aaron didn't possess the authority given to Moses. The green-eyed monster attacked Miriam. I can certainly understand where she was coming from. She was Moses' older sister and had literally been instrumental in saving his life. Now, here she was under his command while God chose to talk to Moses.

The following verses illustrate some of the mistakes she and Aaron made.

While they were at Hazeroth, Miriam and Aaron criticized Moses because he had married a Cushite woman. They said, "Has the Lord spoken only to Moses? Hasn't he spoken through us, too?" But the Lord heard them.

Numbers 12:1-2

Miriam and Aaron had never approved of Moses marrying a foreigner, especially one that worshipped idols. But I wonder if this is the only reason she was upset at Moses. It appears she was jealous of his authority and the closeness he had with God. And, like any human being when jealousy overtakes and we become frustrated, one of the first things we do is tell someone else so we can have an ally. She chose her brother Aaron to be that person.

By the time she got through raking Moses through the coals she had not only riled up her own jealousies but had stirred up Aaron who also began to grumble about their lot. It seems to me that Miriam had quite a lot on her plate already. I wonder why she wanted to take on more. Didn't she have enough to keep her busy? After all, God had chosen her to be a prophetess *and* a leader of the women, but she wanted even more responsibility.

Hmmm, does this sound a little bit familiar? I know it does to me. Because I'd been given so much responsibility at such a young age, I felt I had to take on more than my share. Actually, it gave me a feeling of having control over a situation I didn't know what to do with. Being in control gave me a feeling of being needed or wanted as if my worth depended on taking care of others. Now, I don't think I did this knowingly, it was just something I felt I had to do.

"The human heart is the most deceitful of all things, and desperately wicked. Who really knows how bad it is? But, I, the Lord, search all hearts and examine secret motives. I give all people their due rewards, according to what their actions deserve."

Jeremiah 17:9-10

What does God say in Jeremiah 17:9-10 about relying on our hearts and minds to guide us?

_____

_____

_____

_____

_____

_____

Let's look at Galatians 6:4-5.

Pay careful attention to your own work, for then you will get the satisfaction of a job well done, and you won't need to compare yourself to anyone else. For we are each responsible for our own conduct.

Galatians 6:4-5

This gives us a glimpse into what Jesus thought about taking on more than our share. By an early age it was obvious I thought I was responsible for more than I could or should be expected to humanly handle. **Was there a time you took on more than your share? When was it?**

_____

_____

_____

_____

_____

_____

_____

_____

Many times while my children were young, if I heard of someone being sick, in the hospital or just needing help, I would be the first one there. Of course, it's good to help others, but if we have a plateful at home, God doesn't expect us to neglect duties on the home front to run off and save others.

Think about times you've taken on more than you could handle in the name of being a good person and Christian.

Picture this example with me. You have roast beef, potato salad, cream corn and a roll on your paper plate. It's precarious, but the plate's holding up pretty good at this point. Then – you see a beautiful golden brown fried chicken breast. You like roast beef, but chicken is your favorite. So, knowing it could be more than your plate could handle, instead of waiting until you had room, you just had to take that big ole' chicken breast. Well, as they say, that was the straw that broke the camel's back, or we could say that was the piece of chicken that folded the paper plate.

Yikes! Not only did you have a mess to clean up, but you lost everything already on your plate. **Write about a time when your plate was full, but you decided to take on just one more thing. What was the result of having too much on your plate?**

_____

_____

_____

_____

_____

_____

_____

_____

_____

Was this what Miriam did? Did she desire more responsibility than God had given her? When God found out she had been complaining to her brother Aaron, what do you think his response was? Let's look at Numbers 12:2,4 to find the answer, then write his response below.

They said, "Has the Lord spoken only through Moses? Hasn't he spoken through us, too?" But the Lord heard them. So immediately the Lord called Moses, Aaron, and Miriam and said, "Go to the Tabernacle, all three of you!"

Numbers 12:2 & 4

_____

_____

_____

_____

_____

_____

_____

_____

_____

Oh, my goodness, sounds like God wasn't happy with Miriam and Aaron. Let's read Numbers 12:5-9 to see God's response.

Then the Lord descended in the pillar of cloud and stood at the entrance of the Tabernacle. "Aaron and Miriam!" he called, and they stepped forward. And the Lord said to them, "Now listen to what I say. If there were prophets among you, I, the Lord would reveal myself in visions. I would speak to them in dreams. But not my servant Moses. Of all of my house, he is the one I trust. I speak to him face to face, clearly, and not in riddles! He sees the Lord as he is. So why were you not afraid to criticize my servant Moses?" The Lord was very angry with them, and he departed.

Numbers 12:5-9

17

Write how God appeared to them and what he said to Miriam and Aaron.

_____

_____

_____

_____

_____

_____

As the cloud moved from above the Tabernacle, there stood Miriam, her skin as white as snow from leprosy.

Numbers 12:10

What happened to Miriam as God arose in the cloud?

_____

_____

_____

_____

_____

_____

Miriam's decision to grumble didn't turn out as she thought it would. Does this apply to us today? Can we reap consequences for bad decisions we might make? What is said about this in the New Testament? Write Galatians 6:7-8 below.

_____

_____

_____

_____

_____

_____

_____

Miriam, unfortunately, reaped what she sowed, but Moses and Aaron pleaded for her life and God heard their plea. After seven days of being shunned outside the Israelites' camp, she was healed from the leprosy and returned to her beloved people who had waited for her return. I would imagine she spent those seven days reflecting on what had happened. Miriam didn't get to see the Promised Land, but she was loved and revered for her faithfulness.

Miriam was not perfect by any means – she was human, and like Miriam, Aaron, and Moses we are all broken. I feel pretty sure that probably wasn't the first time in her life that Miriam had grumbled. But God uses broken people!

CHAPTER TWO

EVE

DAY ONE

Knock! Knock!

Don't copy the behavior and customs of this world but let God transform you into a new person by changing the way you think. Then you will learn to know God's will for you, which is good and pleasing and perfect.

Romans 12:2

That queasy stomach we experience when making a decision just might be the Holy Spirit's knock on our heart warning us to slow down and reassess the situation. Is this going to be good for me? Will it enhance my life? Does this person have my best interest at heart? All good questions to ask before we jump from the frying pan into the fire.

I remember with clarity the time we had to go to a hotel downtown when we had *the* big ice storm in 1960. I would have been around six at the time. Daddy and I had gone downstairs to run an errand and I begged him to let me ride the elevator back up to our room by myself. He finally gave in and said he'd meet me on the floor where our room was located. I was confident I knew more than my Daddy – that was until the elevator door closed. I was totally lost. How do little girls handle a crisis? Cry! And cry I did. Finally, the horrid contraption stopped on a floor, but Daddy wasn't there. However, there was a nice woman accompanied by her young son who asked me why I was crying. She was my angel that day. She stopped the elevator on every floor until the door opened and Daddy was standing there. I was never so happy to see someone in my life!

There have been times I've experienced a strange sensation in my stomach, but I'd pass it off as a bad stomach ache or something similar. I ignored that feeling, knowing good and well I should have paid attention to that gut feeling and slowed down. I've discovered it pays off to heed the warning bell. If possible, I now talk over those feelings with others who might be able to shed some light on the situation.

What is your knock-knock? Maybe it's a rapid heartbeat, or butterflies in the stomach. Just know it's important to pay attention to those feelings. Write in a journal about what you're feeling. Talk with a friend. Small groups are an excellent resource for support. A professional who specializes in the area you are struggling with might be able to give you some facts that will help. And most important, go to your Abba in prayer.

And we know that God causes everything to work together for the good of those who love God and are called according to his purpose for them.

Romans 8:28

Application Question:

When was the last time that God knocked on the door of your heart to tell you something important?

_____

_____

_____

_____

_____

_____

_____

_____

_____

DAY TWO

Forgiveness Is What?

"But when you are praying, first forgive anyone you are holding a grudge against, so that your father in heaven will forgive your sins, too."

Mark 11:25

Grace and forgiveness. These are gifts given to us by Jesus. We don't deserve either one, but God gives them to us anyway. And the ability to forgive others is also a gift that he's given us. Sometimes it is so hard for us to wrap our minds around the fact that we *can* forgive anything. When we've been hurt by someone we love or even an acquaintance, it goes to the very core of who we are. Our senses scream revenge or we hold on to our anger and seethe until we become physically sick or our anger turns into bitterness.

Forgiveness is one of the hardest concepts for us to grasp. But I've experienced the healing power of forgiveness. Have you?

Most of us will be faced with the choice to forgive or not to forgive. Keep this thought in mind when making that choice: Carrying around the weight of anger and hurt is like taking poison and hoping it will make the other person sick.

A tragic incident came to mind while I was studying forgiveness – the Emanuel AME church shooting in Charleston. These precious souls were in a Bible study when a crazed young man started shooting those around him. Nine people lost their lives that day. Three women were interviewed afterwards about their choice to forgive him. How were they able to forgive that unforgivable act? Their sustaining faith enabled them to begin the process of forgiveness. Most of us won't have to forgive someone who murdered a love one, but there are many instances we will be called on to forgive: a cheating spouse, betrayal by a friend, or unjustified accusations are just a few we might encounter in our lives.

How did Jesus respond to those who arrested, mocked, tortured, and hung him from the cross? He could have called ten thousand angels to rescue him and destroy all those who had turned against him. Instead, Jesus said from the cross, *"Father, forgive them, for they don't know what they are doing"* (Luke 23:34).

Perhaps there is someone you need to forgive today. You might think what they did was unforgivable, but with Abba's help it's not.

Remember, forgiveness is a gift from Abba.

Application Questions:

Will you accept his gift and let him help you to forgive others? Who do you need to forgive today?

_____

_____

_____

_____

_____

_____

_____

_____

DAY THREE

I Choose You!

For people will love only themselves and their money. They will be boastful and proud, scoffing at God, disobedient to their parents, and ungrateful. They will consider nothing sacred...They will act religious, but they will reject the power that could make them godly. Stay away from people like that!

2 Timothy 3:2,5

Do we choose our friends, or do they choose us? We can and should choose our friends carefully.

Eve discovered listening to a devious serpent resulted in dire consequences. God had plainly told Adam and Eve not to eat the fruit from the tree in the center of the garden. But isn't that just how we as humans react when we've been told we can't have something? We want it even more!

My brother Lee, while preaching a sermon on marriage, once stated, "You need to ask yourself: Does this person have my best interest at heart? Will they help me get to heaven?" Sounds like pretty good advice to me. Maybe I should have listened a little more closely myself.

After my divorce from an abusive husband, I moved into a low-income housing apartment. I met many people who were nice to me, but didn't have the same values I strived for. Because I was lonely, I spent quite a bit of time with my new friends but, before long, one of my old friends pointed out to me that I had started doing little things that weren't in my nature.

One night while talking on the phone with my brother Lewis, who had been listening to a police scanner, he told me there was a police stake-out in the building next door. One of the residents had armed and barricaded himself in his apartment. I knew without a doubt it was time for me to move. Within two weeks, I'd moved in with Dad.

Are there people in your inner circle who are influencing you in a negative way? Look to see if their lives are encouraging you to produce rotten fruit.

This short warning from 1 Corinthians speaks volumes. *"...bad company corrupts good character"* (1 Corinthians 15:33).

Application Questions:

Is there someone in your life who is encouraging you to produce rotten fruit? Who is it? What are you going to do about it?

_____

_____

_____

_____

_____

_____

_____

_____

DAY FOUR

The Devil Made Me Do It!

For we are each responsible for our own conduct.

Galatians 6:5

If you remember things such as penny candy, coke deposits and when the first Mustang came off the assembly line, then you're old enough to remember *The Flip Wilson Show*. For you younger ladies, Flip Wilson had an alter ego named Geraldine. Anytime she made a mistake, when confronted, she would always respond, "The devil made me do it."

That's a pretty convenient excuse to blame it on the devil, although she was not the first to come up with that idea. The Genesis account tells us that the Lord God asked the woman, *"What have you done?" She answered, "The serpent deceived me. That's why I ate it"* (Genesis 3:13).

First, God asked Adam if he had eaten from the forbidden tree. The man replied, *"It was the woman you gave me, who gave me the fruit, and I ate it"* (Genesis 3:12).

Not only did Adam blame Eve, but he blamed God for giving him the woman. So, we've been passing the buck from the beginning of time. It's in our nature.

I remember when I was a young girl and walked to the store with my two brothers and a cousin. We didn't have any money and the candy was so tempting, so we each took a few pieces. When we arrived home, Mother knew we didn't have the money to buy the candy, so she asked where we got it. I distinctly remember pointing my guilty little finger at our cousin and saying, "He made us do it."

Of course, Mother saw right through our lies and marched us out to the car and drove us to the store where we had to go in and return the candy and apologize for stealing. Believe me, that was a lesson well learned.

Have you made bad decisions in your life? Does God hold this against us for the rest of our lives? Of, course not! But there are often consequences we must face as a result of those decisions.

Adam and Eve faced their own consequences. Not only did they have to leave the garden, but Eve would now feel the pain of childbirth (and thanks to Evie, so do we!) And Adam spent the rest of his life taming the land and looking for shelter.

It's not a bad thing to be pricked by guilt when we've wronged someone, but God doesn't want us to carry that burden the rest of our lives. He's already paid the price! This is what the Bible has to say about our sins.

If we confess our sins, he is faithful and just and will forgive us our sins and purify us from all wickedness.

1 John 1:9

Enough said!

Application Question:

Is there something that you've done wrong that you haven't confessed to the Lord? Confess it to him now. Then rejoice in his forgiveness.

_____

_____

_____

_____

_____

_____

_____

_____

DAY FIVE

Eve

Don't copy the behavior and customs of this world, but let God transform you into a new person by changing the way you think. Then you will learn to know God's will for you, which is good and pleasing and perfect.

Romans 12:2

The queasy stomach we experience when making a decision just might be the Holy Spirit's knock on our heart warning us to slow down and reassess the situation. Is this going to be good for me? Will it enhance my walk with God? Does this person have my best interest at heart? All good questions to ask before we jump from the frying pan into the fire.

Eve, Eve, Eve. When you hear that name, what is the first thought that enters your mind? Perhaps something like this: If it hadn't been for Eve, we wouldn't have sin in the world. If it hadn't been for Eve, we wouldn't have to suffer the long hours of labor and the pain of birth. Eve had it made in the Garden. Why would she want more? These are just a few questions that popped into my mind. I'm sure you can come up with more.

This week we've been studying Eve and her decision that changed the world. **What are some things we can learn from Eve's decision?**

_____

_____

_____

_____

_____

This week we discussed four areas relating to Eve's situation: listening to God's knock on our hearts, choosing friends wisely, learning to let go and move on, and blaming others for our actions.

Let's take a look at how God perceives women.

Then God said, "Let us make human beings in our image, to be like us. They will reign over the fish in the sea, the birds in the sky, the livestock, all the wild animals on the earth, and the small animals that scurry along the ground." So God created human beings in his own image. In the image of God he created them; male and female he created them.

Genesis 1:26-27

Here we have a glimpse into God's thoughts. From reading these verses what relationship do you think he had in mind for Adam and Eve? Were they to work together or separately?

_____

_____

_____

_____

_____

_____

_____

Eve was made from Adam's rib next to his heart – not from a metatarsal foot bone for her to be tromped on (from *Blooming in Broken Places*).

This is what Edith Dean had to say about Genesis 1:27 in her book, *All of the Women of the Bible*. "Here we have warranty for women's dominion. The fact that God does not give dominion until he had woman standing beside him is evidence enough of her exalted place in the Creation."

God plainly said he created (them) male and female in his image. Knowing God considers us equal in his sight should empower all women. God chose to use women throughout the Bible to further his message – and he didn't wait until they were perfect. And Eve was far from perfect.

The serpent was the shrewdest of all the wild animals the Lord God had made. One day he asked the woman, "Did God really say you must not eat from any of the trees in the Garden?"

Genesis 3:1

What did the serpent ask Eve in Genesis 3:1? Did the serpent know the answer to that question already? Of course, he did!

_____

_____

_____

_____

_____

_____

_____

In Genesis 3:2-4, God warned Adam and Eve not to eat of the fruit that was in the middle of the garden.

"It's only the fruit from the tree in the middle of the garden that we are not allowed to eat. God said, 'You must not eat it or even touch it; if you do, you will die.'" "You won't die!" The serpent replied to the woman.

Genesis 3:2-4

How did the serpent try to deceive Eve and question God's commandment?

_____

_____

_____

_____

_____

_____

_____

Wait a minute now. Let's stop and review. Adam and Eve had everything they would ever need. They had dominion over the animals, they had all they could ever want to eat without having to labor day by day. The only stipulation was they not eat from the tree in the middle of the garden. They had free rein in the garden and they messed up, right? Would we fall into that trap? Before we are too hard on Eve (and Adam) let's look at our lives today. Maybe we share more with Eve than we think.

Television commercials and ad campaigns do this to us everyday – and women seem to be the targeted audience. Here are just a few examples:

·   You're not pretty enough (you need this makeup).

·   You're not thin enough (you need this weight loss program).

·   You need plumper lips, thicker eyebrows, longer lashes, and straighter and whiter teeth (to belong).

·   Your washing powder is not good enough (you need the new and improved version).

Really ladies, how clean can clothes get? And yet we've all fallen victim of these messages.

Oh my goodness! How many times have I fallen for this trap? Too many to count. **Can you think of some ways where you have let the phrase "You're not good enough" affect how you think of yourself? Write down some ways Satan has deceived you.**

_____

_____

_____

_____

_____

Even Jesus did not escape facing the tempter's snares (temptations) of Satan. Read Matthew 4:1-11 to see what Jesus went through. Let's focus on verses 1-4:

> _Then Jesus was led by the Spirit into the wilderness to be tempted there by the devil. For forty days and forty nights he fasted and became very hungry. During that time the devil came and said to him, "If you are the Son of God, tell these stones to become loaves of bread." But Jesus replied, "No! The Scriptures say, 'People do not live by bread alone, but by every word that comes from the mouth of God.'"_

> _Matthew 4:1-4_

How did Satan tempt Jesus (what did he offer him)?

_____

_____

_____

_____

_____

The wonderful news is that Jesus has already been through every temptation we deal with everyday. Read Hebrews 4:15-16.

This High Priest of ours understands our weaknesses, for he faced all the tests we do, yet he did not sin. So let us come boldly to the throne of our gracious God. There we will receive his mercy, and we will find grace to help us when we need it most.

Hebrews 4:15-16

CHAPTER THREE

NAOMI

DAY ONE

Home Elijah!

For we know that when this earthly tent we live in is taken down (that is, when we die and leave this earthly body), we will have a house in heaven, an eternal body made for us by God himself and not by human hands.

2 Corinthians 5:1

The lyrics to "Where I Belong," sung by the Christian group Building 429, spark a longing in my soul every time I hear the words. Listening to the song makes me want to go home. Not my home on earth where there will be trials and tribulations, but home with my Abba where there will be no more tears.

I've traveled many a journey in my lifetime where I lost my way. Nothing looked familiar. The twists and turns were not what I expected.

So many times we'll take unexpected detours in our lives that will evoke those deer in the head-light feelings. Unexpected hair-pin curves in our lives can come in many forms: divorce, death of a loved one, chronic illness in the family, affairs and many other challenges we might face on our temporary journey.

Unfortunately, I've experienced every trial listed above.

Have you taken detours which resulted in feeling lost? The feeling of not knowing what to do next can be overwhelming. But God didn't leave us without a road map to turn to during those times of turmoil and indecision.

God left us the Bible as our road map for life. He knew life was going to be hard, even through the good times, and even harder in the not-so-good times. His word is the ultimate road map that will put us back on the path that will lead us to him. In Proverbs we are told, *"Trust in the Lord with all your heart; do not depend on your own understanding. Seek his will in all you do, and he will show you which path to take"* (Proverbs 3:5-6).

Application Questions:

What are some ways you can familiarize yourself with God's road map? Can you set aside a little time each day to read God's word?

_____

_____

_____

_____

_____

_____

_____

DAY TWO

God Never Promised Us a Rose Garden!

[Jesus said] "I have told you all this so that you may have peace in me. Here on earth you will have many trials and sorrows. But take heart, because I have overcome the world."

John 16:33

Remember the song, "I Never Promised You a Rose Garden," by Lynn Anderson? Well, it turns out God never promised us a rose garden either - not in this lifetime. He tells us life on earth will be full of trials and hardships. Just ask Eve!

If we go through life expecting it to be all rosy then we will be sorely disappointed. Every day brings new challenges. I remember someone saying, "Don't spend too much energy on what troubles you today, because something will come along tomorrow and take its place."

In other words, when something comes along that calls for our immediate attention, then the other problems seem like small potatoes. Just ask the family who has lost all their belongings in a house fire or a flood. Ask the mother whose child has just been diagnosed with cancer. This life will be full of trials and disappointments.

I used to look at other people and think what a wonderful life they must have, and that I'm the only one in the world dealing with heartache. Then I wondered why God didn't love me as much as them.

This is a lie from the devil! If we fall into the trap of thinking that when we become a Christian our life will be a fairy tale, not only will we be miserable, but we'll blame it on God or think he doesn't love us. That is certainly not the case!

It took a while, but it finally dawned on me that other people went through trials, too; I was just too busy feeling sorry for myself to see through their façade.

We don't know that the young lady we saw at the grocery store has just been told her mother has only days to live. We aren't aware that the stylishly dressed man has just been laid off from a job he held for thirty years.

A smile, a kind word can really help when someone is going through a hard time.

Perhaps you've gone through a difficult season. I know in my own life when I'm going through a rough patch, the first thing I do is seek out someone who's already been down that road and is now on the other side.

He comforts us in all our troubles so that we can comfort others. When they are troubled, we will be able to give them the same comfort God has given us.

2 Corinthians 1:4

Application Questions:

When did someone help you during a hard time? What difference did it make in your life?

_____

_____

_____

_____

_____

_____

_____

_____

_____

_____

DAY THREE

Keep Your Head Up!

"For I know the plans I have for you," says the Lord. "They are plans for good and not disaster, to give you a future and a hope."

Jeremiah 29:11

I remember a hiking trip I went on with my friend Beth, in the mountains of North Georgia. We had walked around our neighborhood lake all summer so we'd be ready for the big day. We traveled two hours to get to the trail that would ultimately lead us to three different waterfalls. We were so excited when we reached our destination since both of us are directionally challenged.

The trail was much more treacherous than our little trek around the lake, and we were both huffing and puffing shortly into the walk. We had not allowed for the unexpected obstacles we encountered on the trail. Twists and turns, roots, hills, and rocks had turned our little hiking world upside down. I was so happy to reach the last waterfall, I could have kissed the ground except I wouldn't have had the strength to get back up.

Naomi comes to mind when I think of someone who had their world turned upside down. When she moved to Moab with her husband Elimelech, leaving all her family behind, I wonder if she looked back and thought that her world would never be the same. Not long after they moved to Moab her husband died, leaving her with two sons to raise. Malon and Kilion married Moabite women. What should have been a joyous time for Naomi turned into a nightmare. Both of her sons died. Naomi was left alone and far from her family. She decided it was time to go back to her hometown of Bethlehem.

Ruth, one of her daughters-in-law, vowed to accompany her. When she entered the town, some of the ladies ran to meet her. "Is that Naomi?" they asked. She looked at her friends and urged them to call her Mara because, *"Life has dealt me a bitter hand."* I think it would be safe to say she was in the depths of depression. I can only guess, but I imagine she felt as if God had abandoned her. I know there have been times when I've felt that way.

Has your world ever been turned upside down with unexpected obstacles? Have you or a family member been diagnosed with cancer? Maybe you've lost a child or a spouse. There are many challenges in life that can distance us from God during a time when we should be drawing closer. It's human nature.

Naomi couldn't see past the present, but God did not abandon her. Ruth married Boaz, a distant relative of her late husband. Ruth had a son, Obed, which made Naomi happy once again. She now had a reason for living. Even though Naomi was discouraged, she never gave up or turned her back on God. She couldn't see past the present, but our Abba could.

Application Questions:

When has your world been turned upside down? Did God work it out for good? How?

_____

_____

_____

_____

_____

_____

_____

_____

_____

DAY FOUR

Keep Your Eyes on Jesus!

Then Peter called to him, "Lord, if it's really you, tell me to come to you, walking on the water." "Yes, come," Jesus said. So Peter went over the side of the boat and walked on the water toward Jesus. But when he saw the strong wind and waves, he was terrified and began to sink. "Save me, Lord!" he shouted.

Matthew 14:28-30

Peter, Peter, Peter. Isn't that just like his beloved disciple Peter to act first and think later? His enthusiasm quickly turned into fear. How many of us can relate to Peter? I know I can. So many times I've wanted to step out in faith, but saw the waves and sat right back down in the boat. Matthew tells us Peter was terrified when he saw the waves. That one word, terrified, pretty much sums up how I've felt at times when the waves of life have knocked me down.

Have you experienced that overwhelming feeling when you've taken your eyes off Jesus in the midst of your storms? Is that what happened to Naomi? Did her overwhelming grief keep her distanced from God?

When we are in the middle of the storm, it's hard to see God's hand in our lives. During some of my darkest times, I've wondered where God was. When I came into the light, I was able to see that Abba had been there all along. There were times I had to ask for help with groceries, paying bills, and clothes for the girls. And even though this is not the way I'd expected God to swoop down and save us, there was never a time we didn't have what we needed. Maybe not all we wanted, but he had taken care of our needs.

Even though Peter didn't always have it together, we can relate to him as a fellow child of God. His intentions were good, but more than once he took his eyes off God. Even with his failures, Jesus uses his confession of faith as a building block for his church. In Matthew 16:16 Peter had just confessed that Jesus was the living Messiah, the Son of the living God.

Then Jesus said, "Now I say to you that you are Peter (which means rock), and upon this rock I will build my church, and all the powers of hell will not conquer it."

Matthew 16:18

Peter was by no means perfect – he frequently stumbled in his walk with Jesus. But Jesus didn't look at his mistakes; he looked at his heart. And he used the confession of Peter to build his church. God can and will use us even if we aren't perfect!

Application Questions:

What weakness do you have to deal with every day? How has God used you in spite of your weakness? (If you don't think that God has used you, ask him to right now!)

_____

_____

_____

_____

_____

_____

DAY FIVE

Naomi

Sing to the Lord, all you godly ones! Praise his holy name. For his anger lasts only a moment, but his favor lasts a lifetime! Weeping may last through the night, but joy comes in the morning.

Psalm 30:4-6

David was no stranger to tears. Many times during his life he wept from the bottom of his soul. If you are still breathing then you have experienced this gut-wrenching grief, and if you haven't, you will.

Let's read about David's grief and weeping in (Psalm 13).

Lord, how long will you forget me? Forever? How long will you look the other way? How long must I struggle with anguish in my soul, with sorrow in my heart every day? How long will my enemy have the upper hand? Turn and answer me, O Lord my God! Restore the sparkle to my eyes, or I will die. Don't let my enemies gloat, saying, "We have defeated him!" Don't let them rejoice at my downfall. But I trust in your unfailing love. I will rejoice because you have rescued me. I will sing to the Lord because he is good to me.

Psalm 13:1-6

"How does this relate to Naomi," you ask? As we progress through this summary of the chapter about Naomi, I think you will be able to see the connection between these two Bible characters. Not only David and Naomi have a connection, but we may have a connection to them, also.

Has there been a time when you felt the pain that David felt? Maybe even at times experiencing a distancing between you and God. You might have even asked the age-old question, "Why me, Lord?" And as you can see, this happened in David's and Naomi's stories.

One thing that helped them survive, while trudging through the slime of life, was their unwavering belief that God was on the throne and still in control, even if they didn't understand.

Can you think of a time (or two) when you experienced this type of deep anguish? Did you have questions for God during that time? And what are some ways you were able to make it through your anguish? Since these answers will only be seen by you, this would be a good time to pour out your heart.

_____

_____

_____

_____

_____

_____

_____

_____

Naomi was a woman who knew what heartbreak was. When speaking of Naomi, she is usually referred to as the mother-in-law of Ruth. There is no doubt Ruth was a kind, strong woman, but we will be taking Naomi's journey with her. Let's open the book of Ruth and see where her story starts.

We can learn quite a bit about Naomi in the first two verses. Read Ruth 1:1-2 and answer the questions below about Naomi.

In the days when the judges ruled in Israel, a severe famine came upon the land. So a man from Bethlehem in Judah left his home and went to live in the country of Moab, taking his wife and two sons with him. The man's name was Elimelech, and his wife was Naomi. Their two sons were Mahlon and Kilion. They were Ephrathites from Bethlehem in the land of Judah. And when they reached Moab, they settled there.

Ruth 1:1-2

Where was Naomi from? Why did her family leave this region?

_____

_____

_____

_____

_____

_____

What was her husband's name?

_____

Naomi had two sons, what were their names?

_____

When I think of Naomi, I often wonder how hard this must have been for her. She followed Elimelech, leaving her friends and family behind and going to a pagan country where they were not welcome and where the Moabites worshipped idols. How frightening this must have been for her.

I see so many similarities between Naomi's story and my mother's story. Mother had severe Rheumatoid Arthritis, which had gone into remission during her young adulthood. She met and married my dad and they settled in Cincinnati, Ohio where Mother was from. Dad was from Opelika, Alabama – talk about South meeting North!

In 1953 Dad was transferred back to north Georgia to work at the newly opened General Electric Plant. By this time they had two rambunctious boys, my brothers, Lee and Lewis. I don't really know for sure, but I have an idea that Dad asked for this transfer. Knowing Dad, I think he missed the country life. I say that because when I was little, we had chickens, hogs, and even a donkey.

Mother left all her family in Cincinnati and the doctors who had been taking care of her since she was twelve years old. It must have been a scary season for her (not that we're pagans here in the South), not knowing anyone and being such a long way from home. Mother and Naomi followed their husbands trusting they were making the right decision.

After reading about Naomi I wanted to see where they lived in relation to Israel.

Bethlehem was in Judah and Moab was located on the east side of the Dead Sea. The journey would have been about 50 miles over rugged terrain. And it would take approximately 8-10 days. To me it seems almost impossible to travel that far on foot with two small children. But walking was their means of travel and that is what they did.

> The Moabites dwelt on the East side of the Dead Sea, and they were a constant thorn in Israel's side throughout the Old Testament history. The Moabites first inhabited the rich highlands which crown the eastern side of the chasm of the Dead Sea, extending as far north as the mountain of Gilead, from which country they expelled the giants known as Emims, the original inhabitants (Taken from www.biblehistory.com).

In ten short years after Naomi and her family had reached Moab, her life changed dramatically. Read Ruth 1:3-5.

> *Then Elimelech died, and Naomi was left with her two sons. The two sons married Moabite women. One married a woman named Orpah and the other a woman named Ruth. But about ten years later, both Mahlon and Kilion died. This left Naomi alone, without her two sons or her husband.*
>
> *Ruth 1:3-5*

Write down the life changing events that happened to Naomi.

_____

_____

_____

_____

_____

Wow – it would be tragic enough if just her husband died and left her with two small children to raise. But in a short ten years both of her sons died, too. She is in a foreign land without her husband or her sons. She is virtually alone without family, except for her daughters-in-law.

I wonder if she ever cried out to her dead husband, "Why, why did you bring me to this God-forsaken land, and then die and leave me all alone?" as she pounded her fist into the dirt. Have you ever cried out to the Lord, "Why?" I know I have. **When was a time you wondered if God had left you alone?**

_____

_____

_____

_____

_____

_____

_____

_____

_____

Read Ruth 1:6.

Then Naomi heard in Moab that the Lord had blessed his people in Judah by giving them good crops again. So Naomi and her daughters-in-law got ready to leave Moab to return to her homeland.

Ruth 1:6

What did Naomi decide to do after her sons died?

_____

_____

_____

_____

_____

_____

Ruth and Orpah were all she had left of her sons. How comforting they must have been to Naomi. We are not given the reason for her decision to encourage her daughters-in-law to go home, but maybe she began to feel guilty over her selfishness. Whatever the reason, she told them to return to their families.

I can see the three of them walking along the road when Naomi stops, looks at Ruth and Orpah and says, "You must go. I have nothing for you where I am going. You need to find husbands from your own country." It took all her strength not to relent and beg them to continue with her.

"No, my daughters, return to your parents' homes, for I am too old to marry again. And even if it were possible, and I were to get married tonight and bear sons, then what? Would you wait for them to grow up and refuse to marry someone else? No, of course not, my daughters! Things are far more bitter for me than for you, because the Lord himself has raised his fist against me." And again they wept together, and Orpah kissed her mother-in-law good-bye. But Ruth clung tightly to Naomi. "Look," Naomi said to her, "your sister-in-law has gone back to her people and to her gods. You should do the same." But Ruth replied, "Don't ask me to leave you and turn back. Wherever you go, I will go; wherever you live, I will live. Your people will be my people, and your God will be my God. Wherever you die, I will die, and there I will be buried. May the Lord punish me severely if I allow anything but death to separate us!" When Naomi saw that Ruth was determined to go with her, she said nothing more.

Ruth 1:12-18

After reading Ruth 1:12-18, write down the decision of each daughter-in-law. Did they return home or did they stay? I really can't say in that circumstance what I would have done, but I can imagine it would be easier to go back with Naomi's blessing.

_____

_____

_____

_____

_____

_____

_____

_____

Wow, so many things occur during these seven verses. Naomi entreats Ruth and Orpah to return to their homeland. This wasn't an easy decision for either of them because they both cried and wanted to stay. But Orpah finally decided to return home. And Ruth makes the beautiful pledge that she will go with Naomi wherever she goes.

But we discover something else just a little bit further down about Naomi. Let's read Ruth 1:19-21.

> _So the two of them continued on their journey. When they came to Bethlehem, the entire town was excited by their arrival. "Is it really Naomi?" The women asked. "Don't call me Naomi,"_
> _she responded. "Instead, call me Mara, for the Almighty has made life very bitter for me. I went_
> _away full, but the Lord has brought me home empty. Why call me Naomi when the Lord has_
> _caused me to suffer and the Almighty has sent such tragedy upon me?"_
>
> _Ruth 1:19-21_

What happened when Naomi returned home? Was she happy to see all her friends and relatives? What did she ask them to call her and why?

_____

_____

_____

_____

_____

_____

Sometimes when we are in our darkest hour, all we can see is the dark. We can't see God at work in our lives, shining his light into our darkness. When we are finally in a place of light, we can look back and see where he had worked in our lives even during the darkest times.

*"For I hold you by your right hand—I, the L*ord *your God. And I say to you, 'Don't be afraid. I am here to help you.'"*

Isaiah 41:13

Write down a time when you felt as if God had abandoned you. Can you think of a Bible verse that reminds us God is present at all times? Such as Isaiah 41:13, which is one of my favorite verses – well okay, I've got lots of favorite verses.

_____

_____

_____

_____

Here's another verse that is very comforting!

We are pressed on every side by troubles, but we are not crushed. We are perplexed, but not driven to despair. We are hunted down, but never abandoned by God. We get knocked down, but we are not destroyed.

2 Corinthians 4:8-9

You see, Naomi was not abandoned after all. Though she thought she had been forsaken by all, she did have someone left who loved her and refused to leave her. Sometimes God's help may come in ways we don't see at the moment. His gifts may not come how we expect them to come – wrapped up in pretty packages tied with a bow.

Of course, this is not the end of Naomi's story. We know that Ruth went on to marry Boaz and they had a son Obed who is listed in Jesus' lineage, so by being faithful to Naomi, Ruth was used by God for the Kingdom. Read Ruth 4:16-17.

Naomi took the baby and cuddled him to her breast. And she cared for him as if he were her own. The neighbor women said, "Now at last Naomi has a son again!" And they named him Obed. He became the father of Jesse and the grandfather of David.

Ruth 4:16-17

I hope that you've enjoyed studying about Naomi and her journey from depression and despair to a time of happiness, and that you were able to see that God had been with her through the dark times, even though she couldn't see it at the time.

CHAPTER FOUR

ABIGAIL

DAY ONE

If the Name Fits Wear It!

"What is the price of five sparrows – two copper coins? Yet God does not forget a single one of them. And the very hairs on your head are all numbered. So don't be afraid; you are more valuable to God than a whole flock of sparrows."

Luke 12:6-7

In Samuel we learn about the abuse of Abigail by her husband Nabal. He has been described as being boorish, churlish, uncouth, ill-mannered, and bad tempered. And that's putting it nicely! On the other hand Abigail was described as beautiful, politically astute, savvy, and wise, but she must have felt worthless because of her husband's abuse.

"You're pretty." The words from my husband would make my heart soar, but then after hesitating he'd say, "Almost." Emotional abuse can be just as bad as physical abuse. It can be unrelenting. How many times did I hear, "Nobody will ever want you," "You're not good enough, and the heartbreaking words, "I hate you."

Emotional abuse tears you down from the inside out. It eats at the very core of who you are. After several years into our marriage I had zero self-esteem. If someone looked at me crossed-eyed I'd wind up crying.

It is plain to see Abigail was used to cleaning up Nabal's messes. When David sent his men to ask if they could come to the sheep-shearing festival, Nabal refused, even though David and his men had protected Nabal's sheep. Talk about ungrateful! Let's just say David was not in his happy place. In 1 Samuel 25:22 he vows his revenge, *"May God strike me and kill me if even one man of his household is still alive tomorrow morning!"*

Upon hearing this, Abigail, hurried and gathered enough food for David and his band of men. Then, she bowed down and asked David to forgive her husband.

I feel certain any woman who has ever been abused can relate to Abigail's declaration: *"I accept all blame in this matter, my lord. Please listen to what I have to say. I know Nabal is a wicked and ill-tempered man; please don't pay any attention to him. He is a fool just as his name suggests..."* (1 Samuel 25:24-25)

Because of Abigail's quick thinking and kindness to David and his men, Nabal's household was spared. Nabal was not so lucky.

God never wants us to feel less than others. And even during the toughest times he will not abandon us. However, Satan would have us believe God has abandoned us. But that is not what the Bible tells us.

The temptations in your life are no different from what others experience. And God is faithful. He will not allow the temptation to be more than you can stand. When you are tempted, he will show you a way out so that you can endure.

1 Corinthians 10:13

Application Questions:

Has anyone ever abused you either emotionally or physically? Tell God about it as well as a mature Christian friend or pastor who can help you to work through your hurts. Seek help from a women's shelter. Don't try to cover it up or the hurts will fester and grow!

_____

_____

_____

_____

_____

_____

_____

_____

DAY TWO

Looks Can Be Deceiving

Have you ever seen that well-put-together person and thought, "Wow, her life must be wonderful?" Or maybe you said to yourself, "I wish I were in her shoes." I know I have, on more than one occasion, only to find out those people I envied were going through serious challenges in their lives.

Many of us are taught from a very young age to hide our true feelings. We learned to put on a mask in front of others, when in reality our hearts were breaking. What would it be like if we could see through their façade? Would we see that the young mother shopping for groceries just found out her husband was having an affair? What about the waitress that just served our lunch? Could we see she's just gotten the diagnosis of breast cancer?

I am confident in saying that everyone we meet is going through some kind of challenge. Some might be more serious than others, but everyday life can be a struggle.

Many who have been abused are exceptionally good at covering up what they are going through. Maybe they are wearing long-sleeved shirts to cover their bruises. Or are lying to cover for their husband who decided he didn't want to go into work that day. I know from experience that the abused person gets better and better at hiding the realities of abuse.

Even those closest to us can be fooled. After my brother read my book this Bible study is based on, *Blooming in Broken Places,* he apologized for not being more observant of what I had been living through. My next door neighbor who had lived there several years came to me and said, "Debbie, I'm so sorry. I feel like I wasn't a very good neighbor." But they didn't know, because I didn't tell them any of the horrible details of my life.

When you see someone out and about, try and remember their heart might be breaking. We shouldn't assume all is well in their lives.

A smile, a nod, or even taking a few minutes listening could make a difference in someone's life. If we take the time to listen, we might discover what they are going through and offer a helping hand or even give them suggestions for seeking help.

Application Questions:

Do you tend to wear a mask instead of reaching out for help when you need it? If so, who is a trustworthy person you can talk to about your problems? Pray that God will give you the courage right now to reach out for help if you need it!

_____

_____

_____

DAY THREE

Can God Use Me?

And we know that God causes everything to work together for the good of those who love God and are called according to his purpose for them.

Romans 8:28

Really? Ask Rahab, the Samaritan woman at the well, or Tamar whether or not God used them. Rahab was a prostitute when she helped the Israelite spies scope out Jericho. She hid them from the soldiers and told them of an escape route. She put her life in danger to help the children of God.

Abba used the Samaritan woman in a mighty way! I love the fact that Jesus went out of his way to meet her at the well. While talking, he revealed to her she'd been married five times and was now living with a man who was not her husband. Later that day, after Jesus revealed to her he was the Messiah, she ran to town and told the people what had just happened. Many were saved that day because of this Samaritan woman.

And Tamar. She had been abused by Er, her husband, and Onan betrayed her. After Er died, she married his next oldest brother, Onan. She longed for children of her own, but Onan made sure that didn't happen. After Onan died she went back home in shame. She plotted a way to become pregnant by Judah, her father-in-law, knowing he would never let her marry his youngest son. She was desperate! She made a bad decision during a stressful time. Admit it ladies, haven't we all been there?

Did God wait until they were perfect to use them? No! Does he wait until we are without sin to use us? No! If he did, he'd be waiting until the cows came home. We will never be perfect on our own. The only way to achieve perfection is through Jesus and the cross. But the beautiful thing about these stories is the assurance God can and will use us too.

Have you ever felt your life was a mess? I know I have. During those times, I wondered how God would ever be able to use me. Why would he want to?

Can God use you? Abba has shown us he can and he will use us even when we are in the midst of chaos. I think the following quote by Vance Havner confirms that even broken things can be productive. "God uses broken things. It takes broken soil to produce a crop, broken clouds to give rain, broken grain to give bread, broken bread to give strength. It is the broken alabaster box that gives forth perfume. It is Peter, weeping bitterly, who returns to greater power than ever."

Application Questions:

Do you know someone going through a dark time who is being used by God? How is God using them? What about your own life? Are you wondering how God is using you in the midst of sin or brokenness?

_____

_____

_____

_____

_____

_____

_____

_____

_____

_____

DAY FOUR

Are You Being Abused?

Husbands, love your wives and never treat them harshly.

Colossians 3:19

I am not the only woman to experience abuse in my life – and I won't be the last.

In 1 Samuel 25 we learned of Abigail who lived with her husband, Nabal.

Just imagine going out of your way to help somebody and you find out they didn't invite you to their party. This is exactly what happened to David after he and his men had protected Nabal's sheep from marauders. When David found out Nabal had not invited him and his men to the sheep shearing festival he was throwing – well let's just say David was not in his happy place.

He vowed to kill Nabal and everyone in his household. As soon as a servant told Abigail what happened she prepared a feast and delivered it to David and his men. When she saw David, she fell at his feet and said, *"I accept all blame in this matter, my lord. Please listen to what I have to say"* (1 Samuel 25:24).

Thanks to Abigail's quick thinking, she saved the lives of Nabal and his household that day. I doubt this was Abigail's first time to fix something Nabal had broken with his quick temper and brash ways. When we read the rest of 1 Samuel 25 we find God does not leave Abigail in an unhealthy situation.

The first step to a better you is recognizing what the Bible says about a healthy relationship. One of my favorite passages on marriage is Ephesians 5:21-33. God tells us what our roles as husband and wife are.

So again I say, each man must love his wife as he loves himself, and the wife must respect her husband.

Ephesians 5:33

A wise preacher, aka my brother Lee, once said. "Ask yourself if this person has your best interest at heart. Are they going to help me get to heaven?"

Abuse has a way of stealing your self-worth. It can erode your very being from the inside out. Physical or emotional abuse can cloud your thinking and keep you from seeking the help you need.

Are you frequently cleaning up messes left by your spouse? Is your well-being in danger, or do you know someone who lives like that? Please take the opportunity to seek help from a women's shelter, support group, or an abuse counselor. It is not a sign of weakness to ask for help – you will discover it is a sign of strength!

Application Questions:

Who can I pray for today that may need my practical help getting out of an abusive situation. Is it me?

_____

_____

_____

_____

_____

_____

_____

_____

_____

_____

DAY FIVE

Abigail

"What is the price of five sparrows – two copper coins? Yet God does not forget a single one of them. And the very hairs on your head are all numbered. So don't be afraid; you are more valuable to God than a whole flock of sparrows."

Luke 12:6-7

Remember this verse from day one? This was true for Abigail and it's true for us. Let's read how Abigail is described in the book, *Women of the Bible for Dummies:*

Abigail is politically astute, diplomatically savvy, and strong. She is smart enough to think for herself, and she is quick on her feet – rescuing her husband, Nabal, from the hand of David. Boorish, uncouth, ill-mannered, and bad-tempered, Nabal makes Homer Simpson look like Cary Grant in comparison. And instead of blindly following her husband, Abigail violates her biblical tradition of obeying one's husband, no matter what the circumstance. Through her uncharacteristic rebelliousness, Abigail's example teaches that the independent thinking – especially in the name of doing the right thing – does, in fact, get rewarded by God.

After reading about Abigail in 1 Samuel 25, why do you think Abigail responded without hesitating? Do you think possibly this wasn't the first time she'd been through something like this?

_____

_____

_____

_____

_____

_____

Though Abigail was probably exposed to abuse from her husband, can you think of other kinds of abuse or mistreatment that women are faced with every day? Example: Being targeted by a boss at work.

_____

_____

_____

_____

_____

Even though abuse is not listed as one of the reasons to divorce, let's look at some verses that explain how God expects others to be treated.

Husbands, love your wives and never treat them harshly.

Colossians 3:19

Can you think of some verses where God speaks of how others are to be treated?

_____

_____

_____

_____

How do you think abuse would affect someone?

_____

_____

_____

_____

_____

_____

_____

_____

_____

_____

Speaking from personal experience, abuse – physical or verbal – can be devastating. The constant barrage of abuse tore me down from the inside out. It destroyed my self-worth, made me doubt my ability to make decisions. I was a broken shell.

There are many reasons a woman will stay in an abusive marriage - one being that the fear of the unknown is worse than the fear of being in the marriage. In my case I didn't know how I would provide for my two girls. One of them was a special-needs child. It was all I could do to make it through another day taking care of her. I was so overwhelmed, especially since I'd been taught it was a sin to divorce except in the case of infidelity. I suspected that my husband was unfaithful, but I didn't know for sure until much later. Even after living in an abusive marriage for twenty-six years and knowing if I didn't get out of the marriage, I wouldn't leave alive, I still felt guilty for being divorced. I felt so ashamed that I didn't return to church for fifteen years.

Let's look at how Abigail reacted to a very serious situation that could have had a very dire outcome.

First, she didn't waste time arguing with Nabal. He had already made his intentions clear that no one was to invite David and his men to join in the sheep-shearing festivities. But when she found out David's plan to kill everyone, she immediately went to work to solve the problem. Somehow, I don't believe this was the first time she had to clean up after Nabal had made a mess of things. She had faith that God would intervene. She humbled herself before David and asked for his mercy.

What are some things we can learn from Abigail's experience?

_____

_____

_____

_____

_____

_____

_____

_____

_____

_____

_____

I look for someone to come and help me, but no one gives me a passing thought! No one will help me; no one cares a bit what happens to me.

Psalm 142:4

Have you ever felt abandoned by him? David certainly did!

_____

_____

_____

_____

_____

_____

_____

_____

Let's look at three verses we can turn to for assurance we have not been abandoned by God.

Give all your worries and care to God, for he cares about you.

1 Peter 5:7

Be strong and courageous! Do not be afraid and do not panic before them. For the Lord your God will personally go ahead of you. He will neither fail you or abandon you.

Deuteronomy 31:6

Don't worry about anything; instead, pray about everything. Tell God what you need, and thank him for all he has done. Then you will experience God's peace, which exceeds anything we can understand. His peace will guard your hearts and minds as you live in Christ Jesus.

Philippians 4:6-7

Write below about a time you felt abandoned by God. I think we've all been there at some time in our lives.

_____

_____

_____

_____

_____

_____

_____

_____

Can you think of other scriptures that assure us God will not abandon us even during the darkest times in our lives?

_____

_____

_____

_____

Give an example of how you saw him working in your life.

_____

_____

_____

_____

_____

On the outside, it would appear that Abigail had it all. After all, her husband was very wealthy and owned much land and livestock. She could have any material thing that she wanted. But was that necessarily the case? There have been many times I would look at others and assume I knew what their lives were like. I felt so ashamed that my life couldn't be perfect like theirs. But is that really the case in all circumstances?

Have you known someone who appeared like everything was great in their life, but you discovered that in reality they had problems they were keeping hidden?

_____

_____

_____

_____

_____

I would say that with today's social media, we see this scenario played out over and over. It's easy for people to take a picture where all is well and paste it on Facebook giving the impression their lives are wrapped up in glittery paper and tied with a pretty bow. We are taught from a very young age to hide our true feelings. We learned to put on a mask for others when our hearts were breaking. **Has there ever been a time when your heart was breaking and you longed for someone to just listen or give you a hug, but you didn't share your true feelings, because you didn't want others to know what was really going on? When was that time?**

_____

_____

_____

_____

_____

What can we do to be more aware of someone wearing a mask and help them?

_____

_____

_____

_____

_____

Every day, more than likely, we meet someone whose heart is breaking and who yearns to talk to others. **Why do you think it is that we have a tendency to turn our backs on them – or turn a blind eye to their troubles? Are there ways we can help and still keep ourselves from getting emotionally overwhelmed?**

_____

_____

_____

_____

_____

As we see in 1 Samuel, God did not abandon Abigail. When she returned home from making amends with David, she saw that Nabal was already drunk from celebrating at the festival. She wisely decided to wait and tell Nabal in the morning when he had sobered up. Even so, he did not take it well. I can hear him yelling, "You did what?" And those could have possibly been his last words because he was stricken with an illness that left him paralyzed. Ten days later he lost his life. When David heard that Nabal had died he immediately sent his men to ask Abigail if she would consider being his wife.

And her answer was "Yes!"

Sometimes God's help will come in ways we never expected. We might not see them while we are in the midst of our challenges, but when we emerge into the light, we can look back and see where he'd been working all along.

I want to finish with a comparison to help you to understand the work of Jesus.

Mankind is like Nabal who foolishly rejected God's goodness and consequently deserved his judgment. Like David, God holds all accountable for their disobedience.

The only hope for humanity is someone to intercede like Abigail interceded for Nabal. She demonstrated how Jesus bridges the gap between sinful humanity and a Holy God. Jesus intercedes on behalf of people and accepts the penalty for our sin so that we can receive mercy. (Commentary from _The Jesus Bible_)

CHAPTER FIVE

ESTHER

DAY ONE

Trusting God!

Trust in the Lord with all your heart; do not depend on your own understanding. Seek his will in all you do, and he will show you which path to take.

Proverbs 3:5-6

"Mommy, watch this!" These words can put fear in the heart of even the strongest of mothers, and I was no exception, and my heart skipped a beat as Erin took her turn on the diving board. But it was a beautiful thing to see the kind of trust Richard had built with these little ones.

When my two girls reached four, they took swimming lessons from Richard, a friend of ours. He had been teaching for years and many of the children in our town had taken lessons from him. It was amazing how he would slowly earn the trust of the children to the point they would jump off the side of the pool and swim to him. It was even more amazing when they reached the point in their lessons where they jumped off the diving board.

Do you know how to swim?

Abba wants us to have that kind of trust in him - trust enough to dive off the side with total confidence that he will catch us. I think the following passage from Jeremiah says it all. Abba not only wants us to trust him in the good times, but in the not-so-good times as well.

But blessed are those who trust in the Lord and have made the Lord their hope and confidence. They are like trees planted along a riverbank, with roots that reach deep into the water. Such trees are not bothered by the heat or worried by long months of drought. Their leaves stay green, and they never stop producing fruit.

Jeremiah 17:7-8

Do you have the childlike faith in Abba that would allow you to trust in him to meet your daily needs, have you lost that childlike faith you had when you were first saved, or have you never had childlike faith in him at all? Take this opportunity to reacquaint yourself with the words God left us concerning our trust in him. Let's get that childlike trust back!

Application Questions:

In what way is God calling you to jump into the water? Are you ready to take the plunge by trusting in him to keep you safe?

_____

_____

_____

_____

_____

_____

_____

bloom where you are

DAY TWO

What Happens When Worse Turns to Worse?

"If you keep quiet at a time like this, deliverance and relief for the Jews will arise from some other place, but you and your relatives will die. Who knows if perhaps you were made queen for just such a time as this?"

Esther 4:14

"You want me to do what?" Esther's eyes grew large with fear.

Mordecai had just asked Esther to go before King Xerxes to plead for the lives of her people. Remember, King Xerxes didn't even know that his wife Esther was a Jew. If she went before the King without being summoned and he didn't hold out his scepter, she would die.

Esther held her breath as her apprehension grew while she waited to see if King Xerxes would hold out his scepter. She breathed a sigh of relief when he extended the golden rod. The worst was over, right? Not so! Just when things were looking up, Esther would have to tell the King she was a Jew and that his most trusted advisor was going to kill her people.

Before she went to the king, Esther told Mordecai, "If I die, I die." Even knowing the outcome might not be favorable, she pled for the lives of her loved ones.

More than once in my life I thought things couldn't get any worse. Boy, was I in for a surprise! Taking care of Niki and working in Special Education as a paraprofessional had taken a toll on my body and I had developed aches and pains. At the suggestion of a friend, I visited a chiropractor. I'd never been before, but what could it hurt? After the first visit, I found out. I was in severe pain from my waist down.

Thinking it couldn't get any worse, I decided to go back for my next visit. I found out just how quickly things can go from worse to worse. By that evening I had developed severe pain over my entire body. Although my experience with the chiropractor was not the norm, it triggered Fibromyalgia, which changed my life drastically. But like Esther, I knew I had a job to do taking care of Niki. If I died, I died. Abba saw me through, working in ways I didn't see until later.

Sometimes, worse comes to worse by the decisions we make, but sometimes it is caused by circumstances beyond our control.

Have overwhelming challenges in your life left you reeling? Have you cried out to Abba, "Why?" If so, you are not alone. How do we find comfort during times we don't understand?

The Bible tells us in Psalms, *"God is our refuge and strength, always ready to help in times of trouble. So we will not fear when earthquakes come and the mountains crumble into the sea"* (Psalm 46:1-2).

Wow! Powerful words! We may not understand why our world is falling apart around us, but we can have comfort knowing God is always there no matter what we are going through.

Application Questions:

When did things go from worse to worse and you felt that your world was falling apart around you? How did God help you to get through that challenging time?

_____

_____

_____

_____

_____

_____

_____

_____

_____

_____

DAY THREE

Looking Back

So let's not get tired of doing what is good. At just the right time we will reap a harvest of blessing if we don't give up.

Galatians 6:9

My husband, Dallas had recently lost his job and was in a hospital two hours away receiving treatment for depression and anxiety. I was now the sole caregiver for my two daughters, Erin and Niki.

Because of Niki's disability, she required 24/7 care leaving no time for work outside the home. I was physically and emotionally exhausted.

It isn't easy admitting we are at a point in our lives where it is necessary to let go of pride and tell someone about our problems so we can do what is best for our family.

I remember meeting a friend one day while running errands. I'm sure the look on my face gave away my little secret. She asked, "Debbie, what's wrong?" With my broken spirit I answered, "My world is falling apart!" She hugged me with a promise to call soon.

It was all I could do to make it back out to my car, where I climbed inside – away from eyes who might judge me, and had a good, long cry. I cried out to God, "Where are you!" Through all the chaos and turmoil we were living through, I couldn't see my Abba. There were times I felt abandoned and couldn't understand why he didn't swoop down and rescue me.

Now, I can look back and see Abba working in my life even through the darkest times. We never went without food, shelter, and clothes. All our needs were met during that time. Did they come wrapped up in a pretty package like I had expected? No, but Abba took care of our needs. Not wants, but needs. There is a difference.

The first step to my healing was opening up to someone else – leaving my comfort zone opened up a vista of possibilities. I've discovered that the closer I walk with God, the easier it is to see him working in my life. Make an effort to walk closer to God through prayer and Bible study and see if you, too, can begin to see Abba working in your daily life.

Application Questions:

Have you ever felt abandoned? Did you cry out to Abba? Can you look back now and see where God might have sent angels in your path to help?

_____

_____

_____

_____

_____

DAY FOUR

Fear of the Unknown

"I have told you all this so that you may have peace in me. Here on earth you will have many trials and sorrows. But take heart, because I have overcome the world."

John 16:33

Wake up! It's only a dream.

I've had a fear of high bridges since childhood. As a child I would dream of a very tall bridge where I was unable see what was on the other side. In my dream, apprehension always grew the closer our family car approached the bridge. By the time we reached the top of the bridge, I was in a full-blown panic attack. Just as we were ready to drive over, I'd wake up! It was a terrifying experience every time I had one of those horrible nightmares! I think the reason I was so scared was that the other side of the bridge was unknown to me; I didn't even know if there was anything on the other side!

I wonder if Esther felt the same way when Mordecai asked her to go before the King to save her people. Esther had not been summoned by King Xerxes in over thirty days and, as we said earlier, for her to approach the throne to request a favor from him was surely putting her life in danger. She didn't want to go! And she told Mordecai as much. Mordecai sent this reply to her: *"Don't think for a moment that because you're in the palace you will escape when all other Jews are killed .... Who knows if perhaps you were made queen for just such a time"* (Esther 4:13-14).

Esther couldn't see God working in her life during this terrifying time, so she was understandably hesitant. But she was able to steady her faith once she made the decision to obey God even if she didn't know what was on the other side. Thankfully, King Xerxes honored her wish and saved the Jewish people.

Imagine you're in Esther's slippers and you're asked to go before the king without being summoned. Would you hesitate? Abba knows when you're facing life-changing decisions. There are no unknowns for him. Trust him when you can't see the other side.

God has told us that he has good plans for each of us. He wants us to come to him for help

"I know the plans I have for you, says the Lord. Plans for good and not for disaster, to give you a future and a hope."

Jeremiah 29:11

When you have to step into the unknown with confidence, God will strengthen you so you can come out safely on the other side.

Application Questions:

When have you had challenges in your life that required you to depend on God because you didn't know what was on the other side of the bridge? How did God help you?

_____

_____

_____

_____

_____

_____

_____

_____

_____

_____

DAY FIVE

Esther

Trust in the Lord with all your heart; do not depend on your own understanding. Seek his will in all you do, and he will show you which path to take.

Proverbs 3:5-6

While reading the book of Esther, I saw two truths that stood out to me. One is the trust Esther eventually depended on to hand her life over to God. And that she did! She literally put her life in God's hands by saying, "If I die, I die." She said those words of surrender when her Uncle Mordecai asked her to plead for the Jewish people, knowing she had a 50/50 chance that King Xerxes would not hold out his scepter, which meant that he could have her killed.

The second truth, which played out from the very beginning to the end of her story, is that God is with us orchestrating our lives. Even in the darkest times and even when we can't feel his presence, he is there gently guiding us along.

> God's sovereign work is seen throughout the book of Esther. Though some people balk at admitting this book's significance, noting that the name of God is never mentioned, it is clear that the unnamed author was well aware of God's providence from start to finish. As God has always done, he proves that no situation, no matter how broken, is beyond his influence. God is always at work, orchestrating with his providential hand and turning hopelessness into hopefulness. (From *The Jesus Bible*)

Have you ever watched an orchestra conductor flawlessly lead a large group of musicians through an entire song or concert? It is a beautiful sight to see. This is how I picture God taking care of our needs. From start to finish, he is there leading us through the ups and downs of our life's song. It doesn't mean we won't make mistakes or have challenges in our lives, but he is there to help direct us back to where we need to be, if we only look up for his guidance.

Draw a picture of how you see God working in your life.

This next paragraph is taken from my book, *Blooming in Broken Places.*

I continued to cry out to God, "Where are you?" Amid the pain I couldn't see him in those dark periods. Now in the light, I can look back and see the many times God provided for us and sent angels in my path.

Have you had a "call-on-Jesus-moment" in your life? Explain how it made you feel when you could not feel his presence or closeness. Think of two things you did to draw closer to God during those times.

_____

_____

_____

_____

_____

_____

Have you ever gone through a traumatic experience, and looked back to realize God was working all along, but you were just in too much pain to see it at the time? Could you share that?

_____

_____

_____

_____

_____

From the very beginning we can see God's handprint on Esther's life. The Jews were Esther's people, and their lives were at stake. Everything that had happened during this period led to Esther's part in saving the Jewish nation and their lineage. The first handprint I see is Queen Vashti refusing to parade herself before the king and his buddies. They were more than likely drunk after their seven-day binge celebrating the culmination of a celebration that had lasted around six months. Queen Vashti stood her ground, but she paid dearly for refusing the king's request. This event opened the door for Esther to become queen.

Let's take a minute to read Esther 1:15-22.

"What must be done to Queen Vashti?" The king demanded. "What penalty does the law provide for a queen who refuses to obey, properly sent through his eunuchs?" Memucan answered the king and his nobles, "Queen Vashti has wronged not only the king but also every noble and citizen throughout your empire. Women everywhere will begin to despise their husbands when they learn that Queen Vashti has refused to appear before the king. Before this day is out, the wives of all the king's nobles throughout Persia and Media will hear what the queen did and will start treating their husbands the same way. There will be no end to their contempt and anger. So if it please the king, we suggest that you issue a written decree, a law of the Persians and Medes that cannot be revoked. It should order that Queen Vashti be forever banished from the presence of King Xerxes, and that the king should choose another queen more worthy than she. When this decree is published throughout the king's vast empire, husbands everywhere, whatever their rank, will receive proper respect from their wives." The king and his nobles thought this made good sense, so he followed Memucan's counsel. He sent letters to all parts of the empire, to each province in its own script and language, proclaiming that every man should be the ruler of his own house and should say whatever he pleases.

Esther 1:15-22

Explain how King Xerxes responded to Queen Vashti's refusal.

_____

_____

_____

_____

_____

Vashti stood up for her dignity and refused to put herself in a humiliating position even knowing the consequences could be harsh.

Have you ever been in a situation like that? For example: Maybe you've gone out with some friends to a bar and they are all drinking and insisting you drink with them but you don't drink alcohol. We've all gone through something like this and it's so hard to stand up for what we believe in. **Write about how you handled the situation or how you could handle it if you were in a compromising situation.**

Esther chapter two tells about the love story between King Xerxes and Esther. *"And the king loved Esther more than any of the other young women. He was so delighted with her that he set the royal crown on her head and declared her queen instead of Vashti"* (Esther 2:17).

It sounds like a fairy tale doesn't it? But the reality is that in no way does it resemble a fairy tale. Read Esther 2:8 & 2:12-17.

Doesn't sound quite as exciting now that you know all the details, right? There are those who have argued about how much choice Esther had over the matter. And to find out, we have to dig through some research to find what the customs were in the days King Xerxes ruled.

Let's look at Esther 2:8 again.

> When the **king's order and edict** had been **proclaimed,** many **young women were brought** to the citadel of Susa and **put under** the care of Hegai. **Esther also was taken** to the king's palace and **entrusted** to Hegai, who **had charge** of the harem.
>
> *Esther 2:8 NIV*

Notice the difference between the words used to describe the king's actions and the words used to describe the women's actions. There were no casting calls or rose ceremonies or consent forms or arguments over who is there "for the right reasons." It was not like *The Bachelor* television program. There is simply an edict from the most powerful man in the world, followed by enforcement.

After reading about Queen Vashti being banished from the kingdom and losing her queenship, it's clear that women didn't have much say.

According to the article "A Journey of Discovery," the harem was a tradition with Iranian (Persian) dynasties and aristocracy as well. Herodotus who wrote in the time of Artaxerxes, testifies that each notable Persian man had several wives, and a still larger number of concubines.

Let's fast forward a little. Esther, who is now queen, is given the message that Mordecai is in the streets wailing and tearing his clothes. She asks one of her servants to take a message to Mordecai asking him what is wrong. He then replied that an edict had been passed that in a year's time all the Jews in Persia would be killed. This was because Haman, a high-ranking companion to the king, had told King Xerxes that the Jews were causing trouble and were being riled up by this Mordecai. The real reason Haman had told the lie is because Mordecai refused to bow down to him. Mordecai told Haman, "I bow for no one but my God."

Mordecai begged Esther to plead for their lives. She replied that she had not been called by the king for thirty days. If you went before the king when he had not called you and if he didn't hold out his scepter, you would be killed.

Mordecai sent this reply to Esther, "Don't think for a moment that because you're in the palace you will escape when all other Jews are killed. If you keep quiet at a time like this, deliverance and relief for the Jews will arise from some other place, but you and your relatives will die. **Who knows if perhaps you were made queen for such a time as this?**" (Esther 4:13-14)

I don't know about you, but this gives me chills when I read it. After reading through Esther, do you see the hand of God orchestrating throughout to save her people? Write down your thoughts.

_____

_____

_____

_____

Are there times when you've seen God working in your life? What are some experiences where you can see his hands on your life?

_____

_____

_____

_____

_____

_____

_____

The words that Mordecai sent to Esther were blunt, but he knew their lives were in Esther's hands. Do you think he did this to wake Esther up to the disaster in their future?

_____

_____

_____

_____

_____

_____

Mordecai's words changed her heart. She thought about what he had said and decided to put her trust in God. She literally handed over her life, trusting that God would provide a way.

Write down Esther 4:15-16.

_____

_____

_____

_____

_____

_____

_____

In Esther 8:1-2 we get a glimpse of Esther's success to plead for her people's lives.

On that same day King Xerxes gave the property of Haman, the enemy of the Jews, to Queen Esther. Then Mordecai was brought before the king, for Esther had told the king how they were related. The king took off his signet ring – which he had taken back from Haman – and gave it to Mordecai. And Esther appointed Mordecai in charge of Haman's property.

Esther 8:1-2

Not only did she put her trust in God, she knew the importance of praying and fasting (Esther 4:15-16). Do you have that kind of faith in God even through the darkest times, or do you struggle sometimes wondering if he is really there and has his handprint on your life? Let's take this opportunity to reacquaint ourselves with the words God left us concerning our trust in him. Let's get that childlike trust back!

Write down one or two of your favorite scriptures about trusting God.

_____

_____

_____

_____

_____

_____

_____

CHAPTER SIX

TAMAR

DAY ONE

From the Frying Pan into the Fire

Concerning this thing I pleaded with the Lord three times that it might depart from me. And he said, "My grace is sufficient for you, for my strength is made perfect in weakness."

2 Corinthians 12:8-9 NKJV

Just when we thought it couldn't get any hotter, it did! That was often because of our rash decisions that caused our thorn in the flesh.

If I had to count the number of times I've made rash decisions, I'd need more than two hands. Sometimes rash decisions are made out of desperation. Sometimes our emotions outwit our brains.

Tamar, daughter-in-law of Judah, (Genesis Chapter 38) is a woman who had been through many challenges and life wasn't getting any better for her. She made some rash decisions, yet she was given a place in the lineage of Jesus.

Eve ate from the Tree of Knowledge, even though God had told her it would bring certain death. Jonah ran from God even though he knew there would be consequences – I imagine he never dreamed he'd be swallowed by a giant fish though. Moses argued with God, asking him to choose another leader – now it took blind courage to make that mistake. Elijah ran into the wilderness in defeat, to escape King Arab and Jezebel, even after God had commanded him to prophesy. King David, a man after God's own heart, killed one of his most faithful soldiers to steal his wife. Peter, Jesus' beloved disciple, denied he knew Jesus three times. Saul, a Pharisee, killed Christians in the name of doing God's will.

If we're breathing, we will make mistakes in our lifetime. But does that mean God labels us as a failure and gives up on us? Let's take a look at how God handled the decisions from those who claimed to follow him.

Eve went on to be the mother of humankind. Jonah was released from the belly of the fish no worse for wear and witnessed to the inhabitants of Nineveh who believed in the God of Abraham, Isaac, and Jacob. Moses, who kept arguing with God, was given Aaron for his mouthpiece. Elijah was comforted by God, and eventually taken to Heaven on a chariot of fire.

David suffered dire consequences for his decision, but God stood by him. Peter was filled with the Holy Spirit and became Jesus' staunch supporter to the point of dying for him. Saul, who was given a new name, Paul, was made a mighty warrior for Christ and went on to be a mighty witness for Jesus.

I hope I have painted a beautiful picture of love and grace. God's answer to sin in the world was to give us Jesus who bore our sins and redeemed us from the punishment of sin and death. I've experienced God's love and grace and witnessed how he was able to use my past to help heal others' hurts.

If you're convinced God can't use you and has labeled you a failure, explore the stories of all these flawed people God used to further his Kingdom. If Jesus had a plan for deceivers, cowards, murderers, betrayers, and the depressed, then there is nothing you've done that God can't forgive or redeem to use to further his Kingdom. He can and will use you!

Application Questions:

Have you told yourself that God can't use you to further his kingdom? Why did you say that? Imagine how God can turn your misery to ministry so that people can learn from your mistakes! Ask him to do that now!

_____

_____

_____

_____

_____

_____

_____

DAY TWO

Coulda, Shoulda, Woulda'

Surely fear and guilt shall follow you all the days of your life. Hmmm, let me think, is that really what Psalm 23 says? Let me go check it out and make sure. I'll be right back. Wow! I had it all wrong. In the 23rd Psalm we are told, *"Surely goodness and mercy shall follow me all the days of my life, and I shall dwell in the house of the Lord forever"* (Psalm 23 ESV).

I must admit though, fear and guilt have been close companions at different times in my life. There are so many decisions I've made that I look back on with remorse. But I love what Maya Angelou said about life decisions, "You made the best choice at the time, with the knowledge you had."

I'd been staying with my friend, Beth. She had taken Niki and me in during one of the many times I tried to leave my abusive marriage. I can't remember whether it was number three or number four. It didn't really matter because when I went back home, guilt would eat at my insides. What drove me to leave over and over? Or, I guess, the question should be what made me go back over and over?

There are many reasons people stay in an abusive or adulterous marriage. But I know what mine was – pure, raw fear! I was physically hurting from the Fibromyalgia and mentally hurting from being broken. I didn't believe I could take care of Niki on my own. Fear and uncertainty drove me back home time after time.

Then guilt would set in and haunt me like a shadow in the dark. Why couldn't I be strong enough to leave a bad situation? Why did I keep coming back to more abuse? Questions and uncertainty would run over and over through my mind.

I remember telling my therapist how guilty I felt. And she said, "Debbie, there will be a day when nothing will make you go back." And she was right – that day did come. But in the meantime, I made some pretty rash decisions out of desperation. I wonder if Tamar felt that same desperation when she decided to deceive Jacob. Or did she feel righteous indignation? After all Jacob had promised her Shelah when he became old enough, but he had no intention to keep the law, and sent her back to her father who had sold her in the first place.

We don't know what she thought or felt, other than her intention was to have a child. This may seem far-fetched to us, but she was desperate – she could not marry anyone else and she would have no family to care for her when she reached old age. But you know what? God took her decision, made out of desperation, and turned it around for good. Tamar had two twin sons, Zerah and Perez. She and Perez are in the lineage of Jesus.

Does God have the power to take a hasty decision you've made out of desperation and use it for good? You better believe he does and we only have to go as far as his Word to see the many examples. So shake off that fear and guilt you've been wearing like a thick coat of dust. Jesus died so that we could have grace. Let's not waste God's gift!

Application Questions:

What hasty decision have you made out of desperation? Has God used it for good? How? If he hasn't used it yet, ask him to!

_____

_____

_____

_____

_____

_____

_____

_____

_____

DAY THREE

Forgiveness Is a Gift

Dear brothers and sisters, when troubles of any kind come your way, consider it an opportunity for great joy. For you know that when your faith is tested, your endurance has a chance to grow.

James 1:2

Wait a minute! I'm not a bad person. I'm a person who sometimes makes bad decisions. I remember the minute that thought invaded my mind. I was in the pantry looking for something but couldn't see anything because I was crying so hard and thinking once again that I was a terrible person for a decision I had made. Never mind the decision was not necessarily a bad one, but rather had evoked a bad reaction from another person, making me feel as if I'd done something wrong - again.

Why is it so hard to grasp the concept of forgiving others or ourselves as a gift from God? When researching Bible verses on forgiveness, I discovered more than thirty verses. Of course, the ultimate act of forgiveness was when Jesus hung on the cross and said: "Father, forgive them for they know not what they do."

Now, I have to admit that I don't think I'd ever be able to forgive like Jesus forgives. But we don't have to do it alone. In 2 Corinthians, God told Paul, *"My grace is all you need. My power works best in weakness"* (2 Corinthians 12:9).

Where we fall short, God is there to pick us up and carry us the rest of the way. Again, in Philippians Paul declared, *"For I can do everything through Christ, who gives me strength"* (Philippians 4:13). Even Paul needed God's strength to do the things pleasing to God.

Holding on to anger can make us sick. We're not hurting the person we're mad at, but rather hurting ourselves. That's why I consider forgiveness as God's gift to the one who has been wronged.

I love to listen to Christian praise music in the mornings when I'm putting on my makeup. Now, I can't carry a tune in a bucket. I can't wait to belt out a glorious sound when I get to Heaven. But in the meantime, I am content in singing along with the radio - only if I'm by myself. Putting on my makeup - getting ready to face the day, is one of those times. I was listening as usual when a song came on that caught my attention, "Hello, My Name Is" by Matthew West. I encourage you to look up the lyrics to this song about God's amazing grace for us.

Aren't those the most beautiful words? We are children of the one true King, and he will be there to pick us up when we fall. If you've been carrying around the burden of regret that has led you to unforgiveness, either for someone else or yourself, use God's gift of forgiveness. Remember, "I can do all things through Christ who strengthens me."

Application Questions:

When you need to forgive someone, do an Anger Buster! Write down what that person did to make you mad and follow that with a prayer asking God to help you to forgive that person. Then go outside and burn your Anger Buster, and as the smoke disappears into the sky, thank God that your anger is disappearing with it.

_____

_____

_____

_____

_____

_____

_____

_____

DAY FOUR

Using the Bible As a GPS

All Scripture is given by inspiration of God, and is profitable for doctrine, for reproof, for correction, for instruction in righteousness, that the man of God may be complete, thoroughly equipped for every good work.

2 Timothy 3:16-17 NKJV

Explorers Lewis and Clark relied on the compass to guide them while they explored the newly acquired western lands included in the Louisiana Purchase. When I was growing up, my parents used maps to get where they were going. I remember thinking that I'd never learn to read a map and wondered how I would ever find my way home when I started driving.

Of course, as I got older, I realized that it wasn't as hard to read a map as I thought it would be. And a map became an invaluable tool to reach my destination. But sometimes we get cocky and forget to use one. It's very easy to veer off course without a guide to go by.

One of the funniest trips I've been on was with a friend of mine, Vicki, who drove us as we headed to Cleveland, Georgia to spend the day in the mountains. She is an excellent driver and I've always felt safe with her at the wheel. However, we passed a sign that said Cleveland, so Vicki was sure we were going the right way. Well, we did make it to Cleveland, but it was Cleveland, Tennessee instead of Cleveland, Georgia. We couldn't stop laughing when we realized the mistake we'd made.

Fortunately, we corrected our course and found our way to Cleveland, Georgia. We witnessed some of the most beautiful scenery I've ever seen between the two Clevelands. But it's not where we wanted to go. There has been a time or two, okay maybe more, that I've veered off the course I'd strived to stay on. But you know what? I've used those adventures - good and bad - to help encourage others who might go the same path I did. God never wastes those detours.

How do we stay on God's path? Did God leave us without a compass? Absolutely not! He left us his directions in the Bible. If you feel like you've lost your way, stop - take a breath - and pull God's compass out. God makes it so easy for us to get back on the path we've veered off of. I love what David asks God in Psalm 119:133, *"Direct my steps by Your word, and let no iniquity have dominion over me."*

Application Questions:

When was the last time you got lost? Were you able to get back on course?

_____

_____

_____

_____

_____

_____

DAY FIVE

Tamar

The Lord says, "I will rescue those who love me. I will protect those who trust in my name. When they call on me, I will answer; I will be with them in trouble. I will rescue and honor them with a long life and give them my salvation."

Psalm 91:14-16

Take a moment to read Genesis 38 to learn about Tamar.

"Please don't make me go, Mother. I don't know Er, and you've heard all the stories about him. He's a mean and evil person. Please!"

In the course of time, Judah arranged for his firstborn son Er, to marry a young woman named Tamar.

Genesis 38:6

I'm assuming that Er's evil reputation had preceded him, and Tamar knew that she was headed for rocky waters. But even she didn't have any idea what was in store.

To understand why she was chosen to be Er's wife, with no choice in the matter, we must go back to the laws and customs of that period. And yes, these laws seem foreign to us and maybe even cruel, but they were set in stone during that time to keep the family lineage from dying out. Wives were expected to bear sons as part of their duty.

Though events centering around Tamar's life are quite confused and intolerable, according to today's standards, her actions were consistent with the standards of morality prevailing in the primitive era in which she lived. (*All of the Women of the Bible*)

Once again, Tamar had no choice in whom she married. The law at the time was known as the Levirate Law. A Levirate marriage is a type of marriage where the brother of the deceased man is obliged to marry his brother's widow and start a family. This kept the bloodline in the family alive. The child from this union would receive the deceased bother's inheritance. (*Blooming in Broken Places*)

What was the name of the marriage law that Tamar was under and what did the law say about marriage if you were widowed?

_____

_____

_____

_____

_____

_____

Do you think Tamar had a choice in the matter of whom she married? According to the customs of that time was there anything she could have done to stop the marriage?

_____

_____

_____

_____

_____

_____

List some of the feelings Tamar might have experienced at that time. What emotions do you think you might have experienced in her situation?

_____

_____

_____

_____

_____

But Er was a wicked man in the Lord's sight, so the Lord took his life.

Genesis 38:7

After Tamar was married to Er, what happened shortly after their marriage? Do you think Er might have abused Tamar?

_____

_____

_____

_____

_____

Read the following verses and answer the questions:

Then Judah said to Er's brother Onan, "Go and marry Tamar, as our law requires of the brother of a man who has died. You must produce an heir for your brother."

Genesis 38:8

Who was next in line to marry Tamar? Was he happy about marrying her? Why?

_____

_____

_____

_____

But the Lord considered it evil for Onan to deny a child to his dead brother. So the Lord took Onan's life, too.

Genesis 38:10

Was God happy about his decision?

_____

_____

_____

I suspect by this time, Judah thought Tamar was cursed and didn't want his youngest son to marry Tamar.

Then Judah said to Tamar, his daughter-in-law, "Go back to your parents' home and remain a widow until my son Shelah is old enough to marry you." (But Judah didn't really intend to do this because he was afraid Shelah would also die, like his two brothers.) So Tamar went back to live in her father's home.

Genesis 38:11

What does Genesis 38:11 tell us about Judah's feelings on his youngest son Shelah marrying Tamar? What did Judah tell Tamar to do in the meantime?

_____

_____

_____

_____

_____

_____

_____

Let's stop here and take a look at what had just occurred. Judah has sent Tamar back to her home in disgrace. Let's put ourselves in Tamar's sandals for a minute. First, she's sent away by her father. Then she has married twice and both brothers died and Judah wouldn't let his youngest son marry her. He had the chance to save her dignity by marrying her himself, but he didn't. He sent her home, empty handed, to the very man who sold her off in the first place. She had no means to support herself, let alone protect herself. Judah knowingly sealed her fate when he refused to keep his promise to allow Shelah to marry Tamar.

Out of desperation, Tamar took matters into her own hands. She no longer waited around for Judah to make the first move. Either out of desperation or careful planning, Tamar made a decision that changed her life and the lives of Christians everywhere.

Read Genesis 38:11-16.

> _Then Judah said to Tamar, his daughter-in-law, "Go back to your parents' home and remain a widow until my son Shelah is old enough to marry you." (But Judah didn't really intend to do this because he was afraid Shelah would also die, like his two brothers) So Tamar went back to live in her father's home._

> _Some years later Judah's wife died. After the time of mourning was over, Judah and his friend Hiram the Adullamite went to Timnah to supervise the shearing of his sheep._

Tamar was aware that Shelah had grown up, but no arrangements had been made for her to come and marry him. So she changed out of her widow's clothing and covered herself with a veil to disguise herself. Then she sat beside the road at the entrance to the village of Enaim, which is on the road to Timnah. Judah noticed her and thought she was a prostitute, since she had covered her face. So he stopped and propositioned her....

Genesis 38:11-16

What happened to Judah's wife in Genesis 38:12?

_____

_____

_____

_____

When Tamar found out that Judah and his friend would be passing her way while going to the sheep shearers in Tinmah, what plan did Tamar devise to force Judah into honoring his agreement to take Tamar into his household? (Read Genesis 38:11-16)

_____

_____

_____

_____

_____

Let's look at Genesis 38:18.

He said, "What pledge should I give you?" "Your seal and its cord, and the staff in your hand,"
she answered...

Genesis 38:18 NIV

What three items in Genesis 38:18 did Tamar ask of Judah? Why do you think she did this?

_____

_____

_____

_____

_____

_____

_____

_____

_____

Genesis 38:24 tells us what happened next in Tamar's story.

About three months later Judah was told, "Your daughter-in-law Tamar is guilty of prostitution,
and as a result is now pregnant." Judah said, "Bring her out and have her burned to death!"

Genesis 38:42

Do you think Judah was just a little too quick to judge Tamar before he knew all the facts?

_____

_____

_____

_____

Read verses 25-26.

> *As she was being brought out, she sent a message to her father-in-law, "I am pregnant by the man who owns these," she said. And she added, "See if you recognize whose seal and cord and staff these are." Judah recognized them and said, "She is more righteous than I, since I wouldn't give her my son Shelah."*
>
> *Genesis 38:25-26 NIV*

How did Tamar react? Did she panic or was she confident in knowing that she would be able to prove he was the father? How did she prove it and how did Judah reply?

_____

_____

_____

_____

_____

Now let's read verses 27-30.

When the time came for Tamar to give birth, it was discovered that she was carrying twins. While she was in labor, one of the babies reached out his hand. The midwife grabbed it and tied a scarlet string around the child's wrist, announcing, "This one came out first." But then he pulled back his hand, and out came his brother! "What!" The midwife exclaimed. "How did you break out first?" So he was named Perez. Then the baby with the scarlet string on his wrist was born, and he was named Zerah.

Genesis 38:27-30

Sum up what happened when Tamar delivered twins.

_____

_____

_____

_____

_____

_____

_____

Let's take another look at the passages taken from Edith Dean's *All of the Women of the Bible.*

Though events centering around Tamar's life are quite confused and intolerable, according to today's moral standards, her actions were consistent with the standards of morality prevailing in the primitive era in which she lived...Second, this Genesis account of Tamar gives us the Bible's most graphic picture of how a quick-witted widow of early Israel protected herself and her family rights.

Tamar, not a wicked woman at all, plays a meaningful role in Old Testament history as the mother of Perez, ancestor of King David. When she lost two husbands, both of whom were brothers, and was refused the remaining brother, she still had the courage to demand her rights to motherhood by the law. After her mother-in-law's death, she turned to the father of her husband. The legitimacy of her action are implied in every move she makes.

After looking at Tamar's life from this perspective, and from what we've learned, are Tamar's actions more understandable?

_____

_____

_____

_____

Have you ever been quick to judge? I know I have. The saying, "Walk a mile in my shoes," is so true. We would have to be in a person's exact circumstances and experience the exact feelings that they had acquired over the years to understand their actions.

> *"Do not judge or you too will be judged. For in the same way you judge others, you will be judged; and with the measure you use, it will be measured to you."*
>
> *Matthew 7:1-2 NIV*

Jesus gave us instructions about judging others. Read Matthew 7:1-2 and pay attention to what Jesus said about judgment. What do you think he meant by this?

_____

_____

_____

_____

CHAPTER SEVEN

RAHAB

DAY ONE

Even Manure Grows Flowers

"Don't be afraid, for I am with you. Don't be discouraged, for I am your God. I will strengthen you and help you. I will hold you up with my victorious right hand."

Isaiah 41:10

Rahab the harlot. Talk about a messy life. According to human standards Rahab would certainly not win sainthood any time soon. The Bible tells us she was a prostitute. Even though she wasn't one of God's children at the time she believed in a higher being and acknowledged as much. God used her faithfulness to save his people and rewarded her life and the lives of her family.

"Have I been in any messy spots in my life?" Yes, more than once. One time in particular comes to mind. I'd just gone through a divorce and my self-esteem was probably at the lowest it had ever been. I guess you couldn't expect any different when your husband says things like, "nobody wants you" or "why don't you go marry someone else."

My life was consumed with caring for my severely disabled daughter, Niki, and taking care of my father who had several health issues. Was God able to use all that hurt and pain I'd been through? You bet! I started writing for the magazine *Georgia Backroads* and it helped me focus on other things than myself. After a couple of years writing for them, I decided to start my first novel. Now the fun begins. Dad would call me from one end of the house, and I'd jump up and go see what he wanted. I'd get back and maybe write another fifteen minutes and then Niki would call me needing help to go to the bathroom. I imagine I resembled a cat on a hot tin roof. But I managed to finish two manuscripts during that time.

Things got tough and those two manuscripts ended up on a shelf for several years. Then I discovered Christian Fiction. I knew that is how I wanted to write my books. I rewrote both of them to fit the Christian Fiction genre. But doubts entered my mind. I kept hearing a voice asking, "Are you good enough to write in this genre? After all, you've been through a divorce and nobody wants you." Could I use my books as a ministry for God? Could God use my books for his glory? The answer is yes he can and yes he did!

And he can take your messes and turn them into messages!

Application Questions:

Has there been a time in your life where you thought you weren't good enough to witness for God? Then go back and read about Rahab. She was considered the lowest of the low. God knew she was a prostitute, but he used her in a mighty way to save his people. If he can use Rahab, he can use you, too!

_____

_____

_____

_____

_____

_____

DAY TWO

Knock! Knock! God Are You There?

Now despite all these things, overwhelming victory is ours through Christ, who loved us. And I am convinced that nothing can ever separate us from God's love. Neither death nor life, neither angels or demons, neither our fears for today nor our worries for tomorrow – and not even the powers of hell can separate us from God's love.

Romans 8:37-38

"God, are you there?" This is a question I've asked many times over the years, because there have been times I sure didn't feel his presence. Even with millions of people in the world we can still feel alone. I know. I've been there.

For the past eight years I'd been traveling to writer's conferences, teaching at conferences, and selling my books wherever it was proper. Surrounded by other Christian writers, I felt as if I was experiencing a little taste of heaven. The atmosphere was electric. I had never felt closer to God than during those years. For the first time in my life, I knew what it was like to have a personal relationship with Jesus.

Now that I had experienced God's presence, I assumed I would always be able to feel it. I had learned the secret. But you know what? A year ago I found myself asking that question again, "God, are you there?" In June 2019 I had surgery on my nose for stopped up tear ducts. I'll spare you the details.

The surgery was successful, but it triggered a Fibromyalgia flare in my face, jaw, and neck. I went to my family doctor who prescribed medicine that is approved for Fibromyalgia. However, I wasn't expecting the horrible reaction I had to the medicine. My life spiraled downward and I didn't think it was going to stop. The physical pain continued to be excruciating, but now emotional pain was added to the mix. I wasn't able to drive for a couple of weeks, was very lethargic, and found myself making bad decisions. (We won't talk about the tattoo on the back of my neck that was the result of a spur of the moment decision).

Once again, I'd taken a detour on the road called life. My writing career came to a screeching halt. I couldn't travel because of the pain so I had to cancel all my venues for the rest of the year. I lost my desire to write – why write if I couldn't market my books? I don't think I'd ever felt so distanced from God. Where was he? Through study, prayer, and good friends I began to feel the presence of God once again.

Has there been a time you felt your life had spiraled out of control and found yourself asking the question, "God, Where Are You?" Just know you are not the only one who has felt separated from our Father. We will all experience that at one time or another. But hallelujah, the Good News is, just because we don't feel his presence doesn't mean he isn't right there working in our behalf.

... For God has said, "I will never fail you. I will never abandon you."

Hebrews 13:5

Stop. Breathe. And trust God.

Application Question:

When you don't feel the presence of God, what are some ways you could draw closer to him?

_____

_____

_____

_____

_____

_____

_____

DAY THREE

From Milk to Meat

Like newborn babes, you must crave pure spiritual milk so that you will grow into the experience of salvation. Cry out for this nourishment, now that you've had a taste of the Lord's kindness.

1 Peter 2:2-3

If you've ever been around babies for any length of time, you know it is inevitable they will spit up some milk. That's just the way it is. It will be months before a baby can tolerate solid food – they are just too young. It is the same with baby Christians.

My oldest daughter was allergic to formula and just about every time I fed her, she would projectile vomit. Yikes! Pretty scary for a new mom, but in comes Grandmother to save the day. With a call to the doctor and a change of her formula to soy milk all was well in Babydom.

Can we be useful as new Christians? Of course! Are we going to stumble and fall along the way? Yes, we will. Growing in Christ takes time. I love to read about the disciples because we can see their growth. I especially identify with Peter. "Bless his heart," as we say here in the South. As a baby Christian he tried so hard. But he stumbled, like we will do in our journey. What about the time he boasted he could walk on the water to Jesus? After telling Jesus he would never leave him, Peter denied his beloved Teacher and cursed when he was asked if he was his friend.

But Jesus did not turn his back on Peter. He knew Peter's heart and his desire to do what Jesus had asked. Instead of denouncing Peter, he gave him this promise. *"But when the Helper comes, whom I shall send to you from the Father, He will testify of me. And you also will bear witness, because you have been with me from the beginning"* (John 15:16 ESV).

If you're a new babe in Christ, and stumble sometimes, like a baby learning to walk, rest assured Jesus will intercede for you as you study in the Word and grow in your Christian walk.

My dear children, I am writing this to you so that you will not sin. But if anyone does sin, we have an advocate who pleads our case before the Father. He is Jesus Christ, the one who is truly righteous. He himself is the sacrifice that atones for our sins – and not only our sins but for the sins of all the world.

1 John 2:1

Application Questions:

Have you seen growth in your Christian walk with Jesus? What are some ways you could keep that growth active?

_____

_____

_____

_____

_____

_____

_____

_____

DAY FOUR

I'm Not Good Enough!

Then Joshua secretly sent out two spies from the Israel camp at Acadia Grove. He instructed them, "Scout out the land on the other side of the Jordon River, especially around Jericho."

Joshua 2:1

As discussed in *Blooming in Broken Places*, we've learned that God can and will use us right where we are. Rahab definitely would be considered a hot mess, but God used her right where she was. The Word tells us she believed in God and wanted to help his people.

And as soon as we heard these things, our hearts melted; neither did there remain any more courage in anyone because of you, for the Lord your God, He is God in Heaven above and on earth below.

Joshua 2:11 NKJV

All the ladies in *Blooming in Broken Places*, were broken and flawed, but there was one important thing they all had in common. They believed in God!

Have you heard of the process of *Kintsukuroi*? I hadn't either until I started researching about broken pots. The Japanese will take a broken pot and fill in the cracks with gold making the pot even more beautiful and stronger than before. If you haven't seen this art before please research Kintsukuroi and see how beautiful these pots become. But for this process to work the pot has to be broken first.

The Japanese use this art to illustrate the brokenness of people. Even though we may go through trials and tribulations in our lifetime that have left us scarred we can come out on the other side much stronger. I heard someone say recently, "No scar is ever wasted." Oh, how true this is. And how do I know, you ask? Because one of my favorite verses assures our scars aren't wasted.

All praise to God, the father of our Lord Jesus Christ. God is our merciful father and the source of all comfort. He comforts us in all our troubles so that we can comfort others. When they are troubled, we will be able to give them the same comfort God has given us.

2 Corinthians 3:3-4

Don't let Satan fool you into believing just because you have battle scars God won't use you! It's a lie. There is absolutely no one who can comfort a hurting person like someone who has gone through the same fire and has come out on the other side. Now go out into the world and comfort those as God has comforted you!

Application Questions:

Has there been a time when you believed your scars kept Abba from using you? Do you see this is a lie from the devil you've come to believe? We see how God used Rahab even during a time she would be considered broken. Can you use those scars to comfort others?

_____

_____

_____

_____

_____

_____

_____

_____

DAY FIVE

Rahab

While studying Rahab we'll see God's grace not only in her life, but the lives of other women who were far from perfect. God used ordinary women in extraordinary ways. Let's look at some examples of imperfect women God chose to use.

· Eve, the liar

· Miriam, the whiner

· Rahab, the harlot

· Tamar, the trollop

· Mary, the demon-filled prostitute

· Martha, the selfish

Are you getting the picture? These are just a few examples you'll find in God's word. **Can you think of other imperfect women God used in mighty ways?**

_____

_____

_____

_____

_____

Rahab was in good company. Rahab, along with these women, were used by God not despite their brokenness but because of it. In 2 Corinthians we are told:

All praise to God, the Father of our Lord Jesus Christ. God is our merciful Father and the source of all comfort. **He comforts us in all our troubles so that we may comfort others. When they are troubled, we will be able to give them the same comfort God has given us.** *For the more we suffer for Christ, the more God will shower us with his comfort through Christ.*

2 Corinthians 1:3-5

How can we use our trials to help others? Can you list some ways that someone has helped you or that you have been able to comfort someone going through similar circumstances?

_____

_____

_____

_____

_____

_____

_____

_____

Have you ever felt like you were too dirty – too soiled to be a child of God? To destroy that thought, simply remember how he used Rahab. She wasn't too broken for him, and neither are we. He is the great healer.

Now, this is easier said than done. I know. In 2019 I was living my dream of teaching and speaking at writer's conferences and had been doing so for several years. Then my Fibromyalgia pain became excruciating, and I knew I wouldn't be able to travel and fulfill my obligations for the rest of 2019. My world came crashing down around me and I was engulfed in a deep dark hole.

I remember asking my sister-in-law if I would have to recall my book, "Blooming in Broken Places?" She chuckled and said, "No, Debbie." And then it hit me. The irony of that question. I had written the book for broken women. Exactly how I felt. Why did I think the words I had written to women going through difficult circumstances didn't apply to me? I knew the truth in my head, but not in my heart.

Have you felt that way at times? What made you think you didn't deserve God's grace and healing?

_____

_____

_____

_____

_____

Can we go by our feelings? Let's look at what the Bible has to say about relying on our feelings.

Even if we feel guilty, God is greater than our feelings, and he knows everything.

1 John 3:20

Those who trust their own insight are foolish, but anyone who walks in wisdom is safe.

Proverbs 28:26

Trust in the Lord with all your heart; do not depend on your own understanding. Seek his will in all you do, and he will show you which path to take.

Proverbs 3:5-6

God knew we could not go by our feelings that are changing constantly, like the wind changes directions. Write down any other verses that come to mind.

_____

_____

_____

_____

_____

_____

_____

In most verses where Rahab is mentioned she is addressed as "Rahab the prostitute" or "Rahab the harlot." Let's look at an example.

It was by faith that Rahab the prostitute was not destroyed with the people in her city who refused to obey God.

Hebrews 11:31

Can you find other examples?

_____

_____

_____

But the beautiful thing about this is that God didn't discard Rahab or her ability to help the Israelites. No, this woman who was known as Rahab the prostitute, would become a part of Jesus' lineage. In this verse from Matthew, she's listed among Jesus' earthly ancestors:

Salmon was the father of Boaz whose mother was Rahab.

Matthew 1:5

What made Rahab different from the others in Jericho? Let's see if we can find out why. According to Alli Patterson in her article "How a Hooker Pleased God" Rahab is not judged by who she was, but her faith in God.

"If you read the Bible, you will meet a God who rewards faith even when it comes in a very messy package. Case in point – meet Rahab. And her faith was celebrated in the New Testament."

Rahab the prostitute is another example. She was shown to be right with God by her actions when she hid those messengers and sent them safely away by a different road.

James 2:25

It was by faith that Rahab the prostitute was not destroyed with the people in her city who refused to obey God. For she had given a friendly welcome to the spies.

Hebrews 11:31

Wow this puts a different face on God's love and grace. After reading this about Rahab do you believe that even during the broken times in your life that God can use you? **What gives you that confidence?**

_____

_____

_____

_____

_____

_____

What were the ingredients that set Rahab apart?

_____

_____

_____

_____

_____

_____

_____

Rahab recognized God for who he was.

No wonder our hearts have melted in fear! No one has the courage to fight after hearing such things. For the Lord your God is the supreme God of the heavens above and the earth below.

Joshua 3:11

Rahab was willing to risk her life for God.

But someone told the king of Jericho, "Some Israelites have come here tonight to spy out the land." So the king of Jericho sent orders to Rahab: "Bring out the men who have come into your home, for they have come here to spy out the whole land.

Joshua 2:2-3

Rahab acted on her beliefs.

Rahab had hidden the two men, but she replied, "Yes, the men were here earlier, but I didn't know where they were from. They left the town at dusk, as the gates were about to close. I don't know where they went. If you hurry, you can probably catch up with them." (Actually, she had taken them up to the roof and hidden them beneath bundles of flax she had laid out.)

Joshua 2:4-6

It was her faith in this God of Israel that set her apart from the others in the city of Jericho!

Can you find examples of other women in the Bible who had that kind of faith? List them below.

_____

_____

_____

_____

_____

_____

_____

In studying about Rahab one of the most beautiful realizations that stood out in my studies is the privilege of being adopted by God. We are his children! He will bind up the broken.

He heals the broken hearted and bandages their wounds.

Psalm 147:3

Write this verse down and let it soak into your mind and your heart.

_____

_____

_____

Here are some other verses confirming our adoption.

"Don't cling," Jesus said, "for I haven't yet ascended to my Father, but go find my brothers and tell them, 'I am ascending to my Father and your Father, my God and your God.'"

John 20:17

So now you Gentiles are no longer strangers and foreigners. You are citizens along with God's holy people. You are members of God's family.

Ephesians 2:19

Dear friends, we are already God's children, but he has not yet shown us what we will be like when Christ appears. But we know we will be like him, for we will see him as he really is.

1 John 3:2

As adopted children of God we have the privilege to call him Abba. I've used Abba when praying and I've heard other people use it. But what exactly does Abba mean? For all things Jewish I go to my well-versed friend Terri:

Abba in Modern Hebrew is less formal than "av." Av would mean father, whereas abba is something that only a natural son or daughter would call their father. So our Father in the New Testament is telling us we can call him Abba Father since he has adopted us as sons and daughters through faith. The Israeli children I know treat the endearment Abba as Daddy.

We may have the head knowledge of knowing we are adopted by God through faith, but let's take the time to study and write this truth on our hearts!

CHAPTER EIGHT

RACHEL AND LEAH

DAY ONE

Ouch! The Green-Eyed Monster Strikes Again!

For wherever there is jealousy and selfish ambition, there you will find disorder and evil of every kind.

James 3:16

Rachel and Leah's relationship is the epitome of jealousy and envy. Their sibling rivalry was alive and strong. But they are not the only examples of envy in the Bible.

Cain was jealous of Abel's sacrifice. King Herod was filled with rage at the thought of a little baby growing up to take his place as king. Saul hunted David like a wild animal because David had been anointed by God to take Saul's place. And David? He was not immune. He had become King and had everything anyone could possibly want - except for his best friend's wife. Envy and jealousy led David to have Uriah, Bathsheba's husband, sent to the front lines knowing he would be killed.

I feel pretty confident we've all experienced envy. Either as the recipient or as the one experiencing envy. One danger of envy is assuming someone has it better than you. Of course, that is not always the case. I remember a time when I had just gotten some help with Niki, in the way of a caregiver, for eight hours a day. But it wasn't enough. The allotted time left sixteen hours of the day for me to physically work with Niki. I had not had a full night's sleep in years. I was exhausted, hurting, and overwhelmed. On the edge of falling off the cliff.

I had stopped at the car wash to have the van cleaned. While waiting in the lobby, I decided to take out my laptop to pass time. A lady, the owner of the car wash, asked me if I was working. "No ma'am" and her reply, "Well it must be nice." Whoa! What did she just say? She assumed my life was easy because I was not working outside the home. I quickly explained what was going on in my life. I must say her eyes grew as big as saucers - she knew she had wrongly assumed my situation. She was so shaken up, she gave me the car wash for free. I must admit, I felt a little bit of righteous indignation at her discomfort. But that's a whole other devotion.

Envy and jealousy are both dead end streets. They get us nowhere and fill us with hurt and anger. In Proverbs 14:30 we are given this nugget of wisdom, *"A peaceful heart leads to a healthy body; jealousy is like cancer in the bones."*

Application Questions:

Has the green-eyed monster ever bitten you? I know it has me. How did you handle that feeling of envy or jealousy? We saw where God talked about envy in James 3:16, but he doesn't leave us without something to replace those feelings. What has God left us according to James 3:17?

_____

_____

_____

_____

_____

_____

DAY TWO

Leaving God in the Dust!

But, beloved, do not forget this one thing, that with the Lord one day is as a thousand years, and a thousand years as one day.

2 Peter 3:8 NKJV

"God, I know you're working in my life. I trust you and have faith you'll bring me through the tough times, but I'll just help you along a little to get this train moving."

Over the years I have learned there are consequences to running ahead of God. So many times, instead of stopping, praying to God, and listening for his answers I've taken off on my own. If someone were to ask me to give an example I'd have to ask, "Which day?" Unintentionally, but none the less, I run ahead of God. Because I had so much responsibility at a young age, I developed a take charge attitude. Some might say I still have a little of that.

I remember when Niki came home from the hospital after being in a coma for four months, I just knew I would have to do everything I could to make her whole. I carried her for many years, in total denial that she needed a wheelchair, leading to my body physically shutting down. When she came home, I took her to doctors, therapists, and we even performed a daily routine called Patterning. Four volunteers would come to our house every day to "pattern" Niki so she would learn to crawl and hopefully walk again.

There is definitely nothing wrong with advocating for your child, I'm still doing it today. But I can't remember one time where I sat and listened for God's answer. I was so determined to make Niki better – after all it was my responsibility – right? I think of how many times, if I'd just stopped and listened, our lives would have been much more peaceful. But this isn't unusual for parents of special needs children. In Lori Peter's story "Season of Silence,"she tells us what it was like when her son was diagnosed with autism. She writes, "I went running ahead of God and left him behind. What I desperately needed was to find God in the midst of my turmoil and heartbreak – not run from him."

In 2 Corinthians 1:8-9, we're given an example of relinquishing and turning our battles over to God.

We think you ought to know, dear brothers and sisters, about the trouble we went through in the province of Asia. We were crushed and overwhelmed by our ability to endure, and we thought we would never live through it. In fact, we expected to die. But as a result, we stopped relying on ourselves and learned to rely only on God, who raises the dead. And he did rescue us from mortal danger, and He will rescue us again. We have placed our confidence in him, and he will continue to rescue us.

Application Questions:

Can you think of a time when you ran ahead of God and left him in the dust? Even in the messiness of everyday life and chaos, what are some other ways you could handle a tough situation? This week, try and see if you can take the challenge to stop and be still enough to hear God's answer instead of running ahead of him.

_____

_____

_____

_____

_____

DAY THREE

Mirror, Mirror on the Wall

Don't worry about the wicked or envy those who do wrong. For like grass, they soon fade away. Like spring flowers, they soon wither. Trust in the Lord and do good. Then you will live safely in the land and prosper.

Psalm 37:1-3

"Mirror, mirror, on the wall, whose the fairest of them all?"

The evil queen, in Snow White, was so determined to be the fairest that she plotted Snow White's death. Even with all of her plotting it didn't turn out so fair for her.

There was a time when I really believed everyone had it better than me. I longed to be like the family I'd see walking down the street or maybe a couple holding hands while walking into the grocery store. I thought their lives must be fairy tales compared to mine. Of, course, I was wrong. No one has a fairy tale life while living in this broken world.

Rachel and Leah are examples of each wanting what the other one had. Leah was able to bare many sons while Rachel remained barren. But Rachel had the love and attention of Jacob while Leah hoped after each son she bore that Jacob would love her like he did Rachel. The race was on. They both longed for what the other one had, not realizing the pain they were both going through.

When Rachel saw she wasn't having children for Jacob, she became jealous of her sister. She pleaded with Jacob, "Give me children or I'll die!"

Genesis 30:1

Rachel wanted to bare sons so much that she was at the point of desperation. She didn't stop there. If she couldn't give Jacob sons then she would give him her maid, Bilhah, to marry. She bore him two sons and then Rachel was happy for a little while.

But then Leah stopped having children so she decided to do the same thing as her sister and gave Jacob her maid to marry. She bore two sons with Jacob. My goodness, this must have been one busy man! After many years Rachel was granted her desire and had sons for Jacob. But, she would ultimately die in childbirth with her last son Benjamin.

Are you getting the gist of the story by now? These sisters both longed for what the other one had. If they were able to change places would they have been happy? I've said many times you can't look at someone else and know what they are dealing with in their lives. The happy family you saw might have just received word that one of their children has Leukemia. The sweet couple you saw holding hands would later have an argument where the husband would hit her once again.

I'll leave you with something one of my psychology teachers in college said. This insight really resonated with me, "Your journey is your journey and you can't wish yourself into someone else's. Take the journey God has given you and make it the best you can."

Application questions:

Have you ever desired to live someone's life other than your own? Has there been a time when you envied someone, then discovered the many challenges in their life? The next time the green-eyed monster strikes, remember they have their own challenges to deal with in their life.

_____

_____

_____

_____

_____

_____

_____

DAY FOUR

God's Timetable May Not Be Ours!

Wait patiently for the Lord. Be brave and courageous. Yes, wait patiently for the Lord.

Psalm 27:14

How long God? How long? I'm writing this with tears in my eyes. My heart is breaking for the pain my friend is going through. She lost her daughter to Covid last night. I lost another friend a couple of days ago. Because of Covid I haven't been able to see my daughter, Niki, for ten months – with no end in sight. Niki lives in a group home and the governor of our state has mandated that anyone in long term care have no visitors.

There are times I want to scream and shake my fists toward Heaven. *God, what are you waiting on,* and then in a moment of clarity I stop to think about those in the Bible who had lost sight of God. Poor David. He saw God clearly one day and then he'd lose sight of him by the next day. David's life consisted of ups and downs. But he wasn't the only one.

Joseph was given a colorful coat by his father Jacob. This made his brothers jealous, but it was even multiplied when Joseph interpreted two dreams which showed his brothers bowing down before him. Joseph must have been terrified when his brothers threw him in a dark, dank pit. I'm sure he thought he was a goner, possibly passing the hours trying to figure out how and why this happened.

In the meantime, along came a band of traders. Joseph's brothers justified their actions by selling him into slavery instead of killing him. His harrowing journey took him to Egypt, where Potiphar, a high officer for the Pharaoh, bought Joseph as his slave. Through time he became Potiphar's right-hand man, and they both became very wealthy. Then when he turned down her advances, Potiphar's wife accused him of trying to seduce her. Potiphar threw him in prison.

But that isn't the end of the story. God spoke to Joseph through dreams and when Pharaoh heard of this, he called Joseph to interpret his dreams. He was so impressed that he released him and made him a high officer. Joseph had a dream that there would be a great famine, so he stored up grain for Egypt. You probably know the rest of the story – his brothers humbly bowed before him and begged for grain.

Joseph surely had a bumpy ride. From the outside it might have looked like God had abandoned him more than once. But that wasn't the case. We don't know why Joseph had to take this journey, but we do know that God was with him the whole way, and Joseph was rewarded greatly for his faithfulness. Like Joseph, we are going to also have a roller coaster ride in this life, so we need to sit down and buckle up.

Application Questions:

Have there been times when you just wanted to throw up your hands and ask, "Where are you, God? I need you." The next time it happens, look to God's word to find the promises he would never leave you alone. Write these promises down and then remember, God's timetable may not be your timetable.

_____

_____

_____

_____

_____

_____

_____

_____

DAY FIVE

Rachel and Leah

We've spent the week studying two sisters. When I was growing up, I dreamed of having a sister. Instead, I had two older brothers. They were mean! But I guess I need to be honest and say that I would badger them to death evoking their wrath on me. Well, isn't that what little sisters are for? I'm happy to say that as adults that stopped, and we became close.

But after reading about Rachel and Leah, I've decided it probably wasn't so bad after all being the only girl in the family. Rachel and Leah would get caught up in a sibling rivalry like no other. What in the world could have caused such friction between two sisters? His name was Jacob.

Let's start from the beginning. Sibling rivalry isn't anything new. It started in the Garden between Cain and Able. Jacob deceived his father Isaac and betrayed his brother Esau.

Take a few minutes to read Genesis 27.

> *So Jacob went out and got the young goats for his mother. Rebekah took them and prepared a delicious meal just the way Isaac liked it. Then she took Esau's favorite clothes, which were there in the house, and gave them to her younger son, Jacob. She covered his arms and the smooth part of his neck with the skin of the young goats. Then she gave Jacob the delicious meal, including freshly baked bread.*
>
> *Genesis 27:14-17*

> *So Jacob went over and kissed him. And when Isaac caught his scent, he was convinced (it was Esau), and he blessed his son.*
>
> *Genesis 27:27*

What caused the rift between the two brothers?

_____

_____

By this time Esau had discovered that he had been cheated out of his blessing. And he wasn't happy about it either.

From that time on Esau hated Jacob because their father had given Jacob the blessing. And Esau began to scheme: "I will soon be mourning my father's death. Then I will kill Jacob.

Genesis 27:41

What did Esau plan to do for revenge?

_____

_____

_____

By this time their mother Rebekah had gotten wind of what Esau planned to do. She pleaded with Jacob to go and visit her brother, Laban in Haran. There he met the love of his life, Rachel. Now this was no hop and a skip from where Jacob lived in Beersheba. Let's see what Edith Deen has to say about his journey in her book, *All of the Women of the Bible*.

This bright-eyed barefoot maiden (Rachel), in her brilliantly colored and softly draped dress, must have been a joy to the homesick Jacob's eyes, for he had been on a long journey by foot, more than 500 miles from the hill country of Palestine to Padan-aram.

How many miles did Jacob walk from Beersheba to Haran? What kind of physical condition do you think he was in? What about his emotional condition?

_____

_____

_____

_____

I know after walking even an hour in unknown territory I would be thrilled to see someone at the end of my journey. And this is what happened with Jacob. When he reached Haran, he stopped by a well and asked some shepherds if he knew of Laban. They told him yes and said, "Look here comes his daughter Rachel with his flock now." Jacob was star struck! He was thrilled to see someone in his family, and it was icing on the cake that she was a beautiful young woman. We are told he kissed Rachel and wept aloud.

This was possibly a kiss of salutation, but he was sure happy about something to the point of weeping. I'm not really surprised. After a 500-mile journey on foot I would have done a little weeping myself.

Since Jacob was in love with Rachel, he told her father, "I'll work for you for seven years if you'll give me Rachel, your younger daughter, as my wife."

Genesis 29:18

Jacob is so enamored with Rachel that he agrees to do what for Laban?

_____

_____

_____

_____

_____

_____

That seems pretty straight forward. Work seven years and get to marry the love of your life. He worked his agreed upon time and married Rachel – or so he thought. Laban had deceived Jacob and when he woke up the morning after his marriage he was in bed with Leah, Rachel's older sister. I can just imagine the shock on Jacob's face.

But this is where I stopped and thought about how Jacob deceived his father to get Esau's blessing. I've often wondered if he thought of it, too. Did he think, "Oh, this is how Esau must have felt?"

Laban had offered the excuse that the oldest daughter should marry first. But that was not the agreement he made with Jacob.

"It's not our custom here to marry off a younger daughter ahead of the firstborn," Laban replied. "But wait until the bridal week is over, then we'll give you Rachel, too – provided you promise to work another seven years for me." So Jacob agreed to work seven more years. A week after Jacob had married Leah, Laban gave him Rachel, too. (Laban gave Rachel a servant, Bilhah, to be her maid.) So, Jacob slept with Rachel, too, and he loved her much more than Leah. He then stayed and worked for Laban for an additional seven years.

Genesis 29:26-30

Now what was Jacob going to do? Did he decide to settle with Leah as his wife or did he work seven more years for Rachel? How do you think Leah felt?

_____

_____

_____

_____

_____

Boy, was Jacob in hot water now! He had just married sisters. I doubt he knew what lay in store for him. Rachel, his first love, was unable to bear any children. Leah started having sons right away. Jacob accepted Leah as his wife, but never gave her the attention he did Rachel.

And when the Lord saw that Leah was unloved, he enabled her to have children, but Rachel could not conceive. So Leah became pregnant and gave birth to a son. She named him Ruben, for she said, "The Lord has noticed my misery, and now my husband will love me. She soon became pregnant again and gave birth to another son. She named him Simeon, for she said, "Surely this time my husband will feel affection for me, since I have given him three sons!" Once again Leah became pregnant and gave birth to another son. She named him Judah, for she said, "Now I will praise the Lord!" And then she stopped having children.

Genesis 29:31-35

But God saw Leah's distress and gave her four sons. **Can you list their names in the order they were born?**

_____

_____

_____

_____

Reading the above verses what is it that Leah was seeking from Jacob? Did she receive it after her four sons were born? What happened to Leah after her fourth son was born?

_____

_____

_____

_____

_____

_____

The saga continues. Now Leah is barren. Rachel sees this as her chance to produce children for Jacob. As was the custom in their time, if the wife was barren then she would present her servant to her husband. And that is what Rachel did. But not before she took her frustrations out on Jacob.

When Rachel saw that she wasn't having any children for Jacob, she became jealous of her sister. She pleaded with Jacob, "Give me children, or I'll die!" Then Jacob became furious with Rachel. "Am I God?" he asked. "He's the one who has kept you from having children!"

Genesis 30:1-2

What did Rachel say to Jacob about having children and how did he respond?

_____

_____

_____

_____

_____

_____

_____

Then Bilhah has two sons. Leah is not going to be outdone, so she offers her servant Zilpah for Jacob to marry, and she presents him with two sons. Do you see the sibling rivalry playing out? And it doesn't stop there. Leah's son Ruben found some Mandrakes in the field and brought them to his mother. Leah was thrilled because these were considered to be aphrodisiacs. When Rachel found out she was beside herself with jealousy. She asked Leah to share the Mandrakes, but Leah wasn't in a sharing mood. I'm beginning to feel a little dizzy with all this envy going back and forth between the sisters.

But Rachel wasn't about to give up. She promised Leah if she would share her Mandrakes with her, she would let Jacob stay the night with Leah. When Jacob came in from the fields she told him she had paid for him with Mandrakes to stay with her that night. And guess what? They produced Jacob's ninth son. She went on to have another son and then gave birth to the only daughter Jacob had.

Finally, Rachel was blessed with a son, Joseph. After years of working for Laban, he asked his wives if they wanted to leave their home to return to his, and they responded with a hearty yes. So, the caravan started the 500-mile trip back to his homeland. Their journey was anything but uneventful. They were chased and caught by Laban's men. After pleading with Laban, they made a pact allowing Jacob to take his family and leave. So once again they started on their journey. By this time Rachel was pregnant again and after a tumultuous delivery she died giving birth to Jacob's last son (child) Benjamin. There is so much more to this story, including Esau and Jacob's reconciliation.

There are a couple points we can learn from Rachel and Leah's story. Waiting for God's perfect timing is not easy. I think I can say with confidence that Rachel didn't understand why she had to wait to have children when Leah was having them right and left. We could even ask Leah how hard it was to wait for Jacob's affection. We don't know the answers to these questions. But the Bible assures us God has it under control. Here are a couple verses assuring us of that very thing.

> *But you must not forget this one thing, dear friends. A day is like a thousand years to the Lord, and a thousand years is like a day. The Lord isn't really being slow about his promise, as some people think. No, he is being patient for your sake. He does not want anyone to be destroyed, but wants everyone to repent.*
>
> *2 Peter 3:8-9*

> *We can make our plans, but the Lord determines our steps.*
>
> *Proverbs 16:9*

Can you find any other scriptures about God's perfect timing?

_____

_____

_____

_____

_____

_____

It doesn't matter how many times I read about God's plans it never ceases to amaze me how he can take messed up people and make something beautiful. Never does it imply anywhere in the Bible that we have to be perfect to be used by God. And I would say this story proves it once again. The twelve tribes of Judah came from this menagerie of flawed people.

LINEAGE OF JACOB

Reuben/Leah

Simeon/Leah

Levi/Leah

Judah/Leah

Dan/Bilhah (Rachel's servant)

Naphtali/Bilhah

Gad/Zipah (Leah's servant)

Asher/Zipah

Issachar/Leah

Zebulon/Leah

Dinah/Leah

Joseph/Rachel

Benjamin/Rachel

After studying about Rachel and Leah do you think you are too flawed to be used by God? What are some ways God could use you?

_____

_____

_____

_____

_____

_____

_____

_____

CHAPTER NINE

RIZPAH

DAY ONE

I'm Heartbroken and World Weary

From the depths of despair, O Lord, I call for your help. Hear my cry, O Lord. Pay attention to my prayer.

Psalm 130:1-2

You know that feeling – you're just so tired and worn out that you can feel it in your bones. There've been many times I've cried out to God and then felt guilty afterwards. I wasn't taught, as a child, that it's okay to lament. I didn't even know what lamenting was. The definition of lament is: A passionate expression of grief and sorrow. To mourn.

And we don't have to go far in the Bible to find God's servants lamenting. The first example that pops into my mind is the story of Job. How many times have you heard how strong Job was and an example to follow? If we read beyond Job chapter three, we'll see a different side of Job that is rarely talked about. And, actually, this is my favorite part of Job because it lets me know he was human like the rest of us. Who could endure what he went through and not lament?

Though Job did not curse God, he did curse the day he was born starting in chapter three. *"Let the day of my birth be erased, and the night I was conceived. Let that day be turned to darkness. Let it be lost even to God on high, and no light shine on it"* (Job 3:3-4).

But, there can be healing in lamenting – relinquishing your feelings to God. I think lamenting should be talked about more and even accepted. How many times do we dismiss other's feelings when they're grieving, most likely because of our own discomfort. I've heard a phrase frequently used today when there is a death, "Let's celebrate his home going," and another I've been guilty of using more than once, "She's in a better place." Even though that might be true, the loved ones are left to bear the pain of losing someone close. Let them grieve.

Rizpah felt the kind of pain that is indescribable after losing not one, but two sons. I have felt similar pain, and I'm pretty sure that you've felt it sometime in your life. If not, hang on because it will come. Right now, right where you are, if you are heartbroken and world weary, get down on your knees and cry out to God. He will hear your cry.

Application Questions:

Have you ever felt bone weary? What experience made you feel that way and how did you react? Have you heard of lamenting? If not, please take the time to discover Bible references to some of God's servants who lamented.

_____

_____

_____

_____

_____

_____

_____

DAY TWO

Why Me Lord?

How long, O Lord, must I call for help?

Habakkuk 1:2

I was diagnosed with Fibromyalgia in 1992 after a traumatic injury. I lamented, "Why me, Lord? I have to take care of Niki."

More than once I've asked God "why?" Why did Mother have Rheumatoid Arthritis? Why did Niki have to be diagnosed with a brain tumor? Why was I in a loveless marriage? These are pretty big questions - and I assure you God can handle your questions.

Anyone who knows me well, knows I am high strung and do not handle situations very well when unplanned challenges crop up. Of course, I don't think there are many planned challenges. I react and then think, which is very counter-productive. On one such day, something had stressed me to the point of tears and I asked God, "Why me, I didn't do anything wrong?" I surely didn't expect to get an answer when a voice in my head said, "Jesus didn't either."

Wow! That got my attention. It doesn't matter whether God answered me directly or sent the message to me, I stopped crying and pulled up my big girl panties. Was that the last time I questioned God? Of course not - as long as I'm still breathing there will be questions like Habakkuk's.

Habakkuk gives us a glimpse of one of God's children asking questions and God answering him without anger. Through the chapter he continues to question, and God continues to answer. I love the last part where Habakkuk declares his faith.

Even though the fig trees have no blossoms, and there are no grapes on the vines; even though the olive crop fails, and the fields lie empty and barren; even though the flocks die in the fields, and the cattle barns are empty, yet will I be joyful in the Lord! I will be joyful in the God of my salvation! The Sovereign Lord is my strength! He makes me as sure-footed as a deer, able to tread upon the heights.

Habakkuk 3:17-19

We live in an uncertain world that may leave our heads spinning. I think Habakkuk's attitude of faith is key to our relationship with God.

Application Questions:

Do you think God is loving enough to handle your questions? What are some questions you've asked him lately? Are you willing to praise and trust him even when we don't hear him answer?

_____

_____

_____

_____

_____

_____

_____

_____

DAY THREE

I Did It My Way

Trust in the Lord with all your heart, and lean not on your own understanding. In all your ways acknowledge Him, and He shall direct your paths.

Proverbs 3:5-6 NKJV

It's hard to make good decisions when we're distraught or upset. I know! I can only imagine what emotions Rizpah had to endure after the death of her two sons.

A couple of years ago, I had the Fibromyalgia-flare-up-from-hades. The pain was unbearable. At the same time my special needs daughter, Niki, got sick. I encouraged the facility where she lives to get her checked at the ER. They assured me everything was fine. But it wasn't.

By the time we arrived at the Emergency Room, Niki was so ill they immediately triaged her back into a room. She was diagnosed with double pneumonia and sepsis and was given forty-eight hours to improve or we might've been too late. Being the trooper she is she rallied and beat the odds, once again. It was a mama bear's feeling that told me something was wrong. Just an example that all feelings aren't bad. But, that's not where the story ends.

Niki stayed in ICU for seven days. This mama bear was not happy. My emotions were entangled like a roll of barbed wire: anger for not getting her there sooner, fear that Niki would die, frustration at the loss of control. Let's add a few more to the mix since these weren't enough: anxiety, worry, and depression. And let's top it off with the physical pain I was enduring. Yikes! That was a recipe for disaster and that is just what I cooked up, a caldron of disaster.

I let all these emotions and pain overpower any amount of reasoning I might have had. I was angry at everybody! I didn't allow any release of information to anyone checking on her. I did, however, communicate with Niki's house mother and let her know what was going on. But she was the only one I'd talk to. Then to show you how harmful my decisions were I told friends and family I didn't want any visitors. What a mistake!

I needed the support desperately, but obviously I wasn't thinking straight. It would have been so much better if I'd gotten down on my knees and ask God for peace so I could make better decisions. But I didn't do that. Instead, I let my unbridled emotions overpower any reasoning I might have had. Believe me when I say there were some not- so- good outcomes because of my rash decision making. I regret those decisions.

Emotions have a way of clouding our judgment. God gave us a compass to go by when this occurs – his Word.

For we walk by faith, not by sight.

2 Corinthians 5:7 NKJV

He who is slow to anger is better than the mighty; and he who rules his spirit better than he who takes a city.

Proverbs 16:32 NKJV

This next verse reminds us how God wants us to respond to out-of-control feelings.

Be anxious for nothing, but in everything by prayer and supplication, with thanksgiving, let your requests be made known to God; and the peace of God, which surpasses all understanding, will guard your hearts and minds through Christ Jesus.

Philippians 4:6-7 NKJV

Application Questions:

Have you had to deal with conflicting emotions lately? Are you the one in the back waving your had vigorously? Don't forget the compass God gave us to go by when those emotions cloud our judgment.

_____

_____

_____

_____

_____

DAY FOUR

That Dirty Four-Letter Word – Grief

Grieving can be a lonely place. The funeral is over, all the casseroles have been put in the freezer, and your friends and family have returned to their lives. You tell them you'll be fine. But when you wave good-bye to the last guest you look around at the empty house. The silence is deafening. Grief is something that can't be turned off and on like a light switch.

But grieving isn't a bad thing and can help the healing process. There are many examples in the Bible of people grieving. Their customs were somewhat different from ours today. When I wanted to research how the Jewish people grieved in Jesus' time, I went to my friend and fellow writer, Terri Gillespie, who is familiar with Jewish traditions.

> Common ways to show mourning in biblical times included weeping and crying loudly. Also, beating the breast, bowing the head, and fasting were often part of the mourning process. Sometimes, mourners would sprinkle ashes, dust, or dirt on themselves and tear their clothing. Mourning was a time to remove jewelry and other ornamentation, walk barefoot, and possibly wear a goat-hair garment, called sackcloth.
>
> Typically, mourners would come to the bereaved's home and bring food – a very Jewish thing to do. The goal was to encourage the grieving to eat, even in their sorrow. Shiva (Hebrew term: seven) is the week-long mourning period in Judaism for first degree relatives. The ritual is referred to as "sitting Shiva" in English. Sitting Shiva for someone is considered a "mitzvah" a good deed.

She goes on to tell me when both her sister and her sister-in-law died within months of each other, friends drove from Pennsylvania to Georgia to sit shiva. "They cooked for us, sat and let us talk, cry and laugh. We watched movies, prayed, and did more talking. They never knew our sisters, but they knew we were here in Georgia without family, so they came!"

Application Questions:

Have you lost someone in your life who you grieved deeply for? What are some ways friends and family showed their care and concern? Do you sometimes feel uncomfortable around a friend or loved one who has just lost someone close? Ask what they need and let them grieve. Perhaps they just need someone to listen, laugh, cry and pray with them.

_____

_____

_____

_____

_____

_____

_____

_____

_____

_____

DAY FIVE

Rizpah

Have you ever cried so hard that you couldn't get your breath? I have. And I'm pretty sure Rizpah did, too. Rizpah is one of those women in the Bible that doesn't get a lot of air time – but she's a mother with a broken heart.

To learn Rizpah's story read 2 Samuel 21.

To understand Rizpah's broken heart we need back story. At this point King Saul and his son Jonathan had been killed in battle. David was destined to be king. After Saul's death two of his heirs use Rizpah as a pawn because she was a concubine of the King.

In her lifetime, Rizpah also played a part in the struggle for power within the monarchy. When the sons of Saul's wife, Queen Ahinoam, die in battle, just one legitimate heir to the throne remains – Ishbaal. He had been too young to fight and was still too young to rule, so Saul's uncle and general, Abner, comes to act as a regent. When he can't control the throne as he would like, Abner takes Rizpah as his own concubine, hoping that if he can have a son with Rizpah, the royal concubine, then he has a remote claim to the throne. (*All of the Women of the Bible*)

As the war between the house of Saul and the house of David went on, Abner became a powerful leader among those loyal to Saul. One day Ishbosheth, Saul's son, accused Abner of sleeping with one of his father's concubines, a woman named Rizpah, daughter of Aiah.

2 Samuel 3:6-7

We don't know what Rizpah's life was like up to this point, but we do know she had no choice in the matter. She was thrown into the middle of a battle for the throne of her dead husband. She is in the grieving process when Abner decides to use her as a bargaining chip for the throne.

Have you been thrown in the middle of someone else's battle? How did that make you feel? Do you think Rizpah might have had some of the same feelings?

_____

_____

_____

_____

_____

Saul and David had a tumultuous relationship, and Saul held tightly to the throne. He didn't want to surrender it to David. In 1 Samuel 13 we read about King Saul's disobedience to God that would ultimately lead to his death.

> *Just as Saul was finishing with the burnt offering, Samuel arrived. Saul went out to meet and welcome him. But Samuel said, "What is this you have done?" Saul replied, "I saw my men scattering from me, and you didn't arrive when you said you would, and the Philistines are at Micmash ready for battle. So I said, "The Philistines are ready to march against us at Gilgal, and I haven't even asked for the Lord's help! So I felt compelled to offer the burnt offering myself before you came." "How foolish!" Samuel exclaimed. "You have not kept the command the Lord your God gave you."...*
>
> *1 Samuel 13:10-13*

What did Saul do that displeased God? Have you ever been in a situation where you let fear step in and influence your decision? What was the result?

_____

_____

_____

_____

_____

We can read about Saul's death in 1 Samuel 31.

Now the Philistines attacked Israel, and the men of Israel fled before them. Many were slaughtered on the slopes of Mount Gilboa. The Philistines closed in on Saul and his three sons, and they killed three of his sons – Jonathan, Abinadab, and Malkishua. The fighting grew very fierce around Saul, and the Philistine archers caught up with him and wounded him severely.

Saul groaned to his armor bearer, "Take the sword and kill me before these pagan Philistines come to run me through and taunt and torture me." But his armor bearer was afraid and would not do it. So Saul took his own sword and fell on it.

1 Samuel 31:1-4

How did Saul die? Which three sons were killed with him in battle?

_____

_____

_____

_____

Now we've come full circle back to Rizpah and Saul's son Ishbaal who accused Abner of taking King Saul's concubine for his own. Rizpah has already been through so much. But losing Saul was just the beginning of the troubles she would endure. Rizpah will lose her two sons Armoni and Mephibosheth to an act of war that must have seemed so unjust to her.

There had been a three-year famine during David's reign. He asked the Lord why they were having this famine and the Lord told him, *"The famine has come because Saul and his family are guilty of murdering the Gibeonites"* (2 Samuel 21:1).

David approached the Gibeonites and asked how he could make amends for Saul's disobedience.

Then they replied, "It was Saul who planned to destroy us, to keep us from having any place at all in the territory of Israel. So let seven of Saul's sons be handed over to us, and we will execute them before the Lord at Gibeon, on the mountain of the Lord."

2 Samuel 21:3-6

How do the Gibeonites respond to David?

_____

_____

_____

_____

Armoni and Mephibosheth, Rizpah's sons, were included in the seven sons that were executed.

Do you think Rizpah cried out, "Why, God, why? Why were my sons sacrificed for the sins of others?" Have you ever cried out to God, "Why, Lord?" What was one of those times? What are some things you did to help you through those times?

_____

_____

_____

_____

_____

_____

_____

Then Rizpah, daughter of Aiah, the mother of the two men, spread burlap on a rock and stayed there the entire harvest season. She prevented the scavenger birds from tearing at their bodies during the day and stopped wild animals from eating them at night.

2 Samuel 21:10

What did Rizpah do after her two sons were killed? What were your first thoughts when you read this?

_____

_____

_____

_____

_____

The Bible doesn't tell us what Rizpah was thinking, we have to fill in those blanks. But just the fact that she stayed with their bodies to keep the wild animals from them shows she had faith God would send help. I can only imagine what she went through as people passed by and looked at her guarding her son's bodies. I wonder if they whispered to each other, "That's _crazy_ Rizpah."

I know this can happen. I experienced this recently. I fell on the curb at the mall a few weeks ago and waited on the sidewalk for someone to help me. Finally, three young women came to my rescue. As I hugged them with gratefulness, one said, "You won't believe how many people walked by you." I was astounded but shouldn't have been. My daughter Niki is in a wheelchair, and I can count on both hands how many times people offered to open the door for us.

As I was reading about this loving mother, many thoughts ran through my mind. One question I have asked many times is "Why Niki?" She was a happy, chubby little three-year-old when she was diagnosed with her brain tumor. After surgery and radiation, she was left severely disabled. There is no response on earth that can answer my question. And Rizpah may have felt the same way. You may have felt this way at one time or another. If not then fasten your seat belt, because you will sometime in your life. I've realized the hard way there are just going to be things we don't understand on earth. And God tells us that. Let's look at what the Bible has to say about unanswered questions.

"My thoughts are nothing like your thoughts," says the Lord. "And my ways are far beyond anything you could imagine. For just as the heavens are higher than the earth, so my ways are higher than your ways and my thoughts higher than your thoughts."

Isaiah 55:8-9

What do you think this means?

_____

_____

_____

_____

_____

God clearly tells us we are not capable of understanding his ways. And Isaiah is not the only one who did not understand God's ways. Let's take a look at Habakkuk's pleading questions.

How long, O Lord, must I call for help? But you do not listen! "Violence is everywhere!" I cry, but you do not come to save. Must I forever see these evil deeds? Why must I watch all this misery? Wherever I look, I see destruction and violence. I am surrounded by people who love to argue and fight. The law has become paralyzed, and there is no justice in the courts. The wicked far outnumber the righteous, so that justice has become perverted.

Habakkuk 1:1-4

After reading Habakkuk's pleas can you relate to anything he's saying? Does it look a little like the times we are going through now? Can you see we are not the first generation to go through things we don't understand?

_____

_____

_____

_____

_____

Now let's read God's reply to Habakkuk.

The Lord replied, "Look around you at the nations; look and be amazed! For I am doing something in your own day, something you wouldn't believe even if someone told you about it...."

Habakkuk 1:5

In your own words, what does he say to Habakkuk? From reading God's reply do you think Habakkuk was capable of understanding God's ways even if God told him what he was doing?

_____

_____

_____

_____

_____

_____

_____

Let's return to Rizpah guarding her dead son's bodies from the wild animals. She didn't waiver in her watch, yes she may have asked, "Why, Lord?" But the fact that she continued her vigilant watch over her sons speaks louder than her words. And her sacrifice was not in vain.

When David learned what Rizpah, Saul's concubine, had done, he went to the people of Jabesh-gilead and retrieved the bones of Saul and his son Jonathan. So David obtained the bones of Saul and Jonathan, as well as the bones of the men the Gibeonites had executed. Then the king ordered that they bury the bones in the tomb of Kish, Saul's father, at the town of Zelda in the land of Benjamin. After that, God ended the famine in the land.

2 Samuel 21:11-14

My hope, after studying Rizpah, is that you understand there will be unanswered questions while we inhabit our earthly bodies. In no way does this reflect God's love for you. Take a few minutes to write down some verses that assure you of God's love, that he is still on the throne, and then meditate on them whenever you have a broken heart.

_____

_____

_____

_____

_____

_____

_____

_____

_____

_____

_____

_____

CHAPTER TEN

THE SAMARITAN WOMAN

DAY ONE

Never Left Alone

"...Be sure of this: I am with you always, even to the end of the age."

Matthew 28:20

Divorced! Oh, my goodness. Could I ever show my face again in church? I didn't for fifteen years.

Why? Because of the shame I felt. The church I grew up in frowned upon divorce except in cases of infidelity. Which was true in my case, but I didn't know for sure until after the divorce.

Shame was one of the reasons I stayed in an abusive marriage for twenty-six years. Mine isn't the only case of feeling shamed at something we've done. When Mother was very sick towards the end of her life, one of the doctors was going over her history with me when he mentioned her first marriage. What? First marriage? Was he crazy? Mother had never been married to anybody but Dad. Right?

So I went to Mother and asked her. She told me when she was a young girl, she had married someone who was in the Navy, and he had cheated on her while he was overseas. My heart sank – not because she'd been married before – but because she was so ashamed, she felt she had to hide it all those years.

I wonder if this is how the Samaritan woman felt when she went to get water from the well, in the heat of the day, so she wouldn't have to endure the stares and gossip?

So many times I've been quick to judge and point a finger at someone else for their short-comings, seemingly forgetting my own. Maybe you've been a little too quick to judge someone. I liked the WWJD (What Would Jesus Do) jewelry that people used to wear. It's a question that should make us stop and think before making assumptions.

What *did* Jesus do when he met the Samaritan woman at the well? Did he scold her, shame her, or tell her she had no chance of being saved? No. He didn't. Instead, he used her as a vessel to share the Good News with others in her town.

That's what Jesus does. He uses the broken as his mediator to others who are broken. The healthy don't need a doctor.

Application Questions:

Have you ever felt so broken that you thought God could not use you? Could you relate to the Samaritan woman at the well? Remember her story as an example of how God can and will use you even in your darkest times!

_____

_____

_____

_____

_____

_____

_____

DAY TWO

Oops! I Messed Up Again

But if we confess our sins to him, he is faithful and just to forgive us our sins and cleanse us from all wickedness.

1 John 1:9

Oops! I'd messed up again. Oh well, it wasn't the first time and surely wouldn't be the last time I made a mess of things, then had to live with the results. And that's just in one day.

Yes, I was trying to be funny, but it's not far from the truth. There are consequences to every action - good or bad. And when we act before we think many times we will have unwanted consequences. Maybe we've spoken in anger to a friend, and now she won't talk to us. Or maybe we even thought we were doing a good deed by getting involved in a situation of a loved one - and it backfired. Even though we don't realize it as such at the time, it is really more about control. And it was not our situation to control.

But the good news is we are in very good company and God does not hold our inequities against us. I'm in a Bible study group studying *Jonah* by Priscilla Shirer. Who would have thought you could make an entire study out of his story. It's amazing how many lessons we can learn from Jonah's mistakes. One of the main points in this study is how are we going to react to God's interruptions in our lives.

God told Jonah, *"Go to the great city of Nineveh and preach against it, because its wickedness has come up before me"* (Jonah 1:1 NIV). The people of Nineveh were enemies of the Jews and Jonah didn't think that was such a good idea. Maybe he was afraid, maybe he didn't believe they deserved being saved. Whatever the reason, he fled across the sea to Tarshish, in the opposite direction of Nineveh. Yikes! Was that a mistake? I find it interesting that Jonah knew about God's omnipotence but he thought he could hide from God.

We know as the story progresses he takes a boat to Tarshish and goes down in the belly of the ship and goes to sleep. It seems as if Jonah was able to put God completely out of his thoughts - that is for a while. God made a great storm appear that caused the men to fear for their lives. At Jonah's request they threw him into the sea and it immediately became calm. Then as we've heard since childhood, a big fish swallowed Jonah.

That is a pretty dire consequence to Jonah's decision. We may not be swallowed by a big fish for three days and nights for our decisions, but rest assured we all have to live with decisions made without seeking God's answer first. As a result of the Samaritan woman's lifestyle, she lived with ridicule from others. So much so that she came to the well to draw water at the hottest time of the day to avoid them. Jesus didn't use her lifestyle against her, he used it to let her know she was in the presence of the Messiah. Even though her life was far from perfect, Jesus chose to use her that day. *"Many of the Samaritans from the town believed in him because the woman had said, 'He told me everything I ever did'"* (John 4:39).

Yep, we may have messed up, but God can take our messes and use them for his glory!

Application Questions:

Why do you think Jesus went out of his way to meet the Samaritan woman? After reading this woman's story, do you believe that God has a testimony you can use to help others? Think of ways your life experiences can be used to help others.

_____

_____

_____

_____

_____

_____

_____

_____

DAY THREE

Lest You Be Judged

"Do not judge others, and you will not be judged."

Matthew 7:1

Jesus never withheld his love or goodness to anyone because of their behavior. If that were true where would we as Gentiles be?

Many times after Jesus healed an infirmity, then, and only then did he tell the person to go and sin no more. Their healing wasn't dependent on their past life. I think it's obvious the Samaritan woman at the well had been judged and ostracized for her life choices. Jesus didn't choose one of the self-righteous to have a one-on-one conversation with. But he did share he was the Messiah, with the Samaritan woman and used her to further his kingdom.

It's human nature to judge someone even before we know their full story – sometimes even by how they look. I love the rest of the passage that starts off in Matthew 7:

> *"For you will be treated as you treat others. The standard you use in judging is the standard by which you will be judged. And why worry about a speck in your friend's eye when you have a log in your own? How can you think of saying to your friend, 'Let me help you get rid of that speck in your eye,' when you can't see past the log in your own eye?"*

Matthew 7:2-4

Jesus didn't mince words. We are called to love others and leave the judging up to God. As humans we will undoubtedly be quick to judge others because that is what our flawed nature does.

One example comes to mind when I was too quick to judge. I have been to many venues where I sell my books. I love to stop people and share my writing journey with them. But there has been more than one occasion I've made a quick judgment and assumed that person probably wasn't a reader. And you know what? I've been wrong a lot more times than I've been right. I learned very quickly not to judge potential customers on their looks. How arrogant of me.

Now, you've probably never experienced a time when you were way too quick to judge someone else. But, just in case you have, like me, take a step back and remember we do not know that person's background or story. God does! Take a deep breath, step back and remember, the standard by which you judge will be the standard by which you will be judged.

Application Questions:

Have you ever been quick to judge someone? Have there been times in your life when others have quickly judged you? How did that make you feel? The next time you are tempted to judge someone count to ten and remember those feelings you experienced when you were judged.

_____

_____

_____

_____

_____

_____

_____

_____

_____

_____

DAY FOUR

Never Too Late

Jesus replied, "Anyone who drinks this water will soon become thirsty again. But those who drink the water I give will never be thirsty again. It becomes a fresh, bubbling spring within them, giving them eternal life."

John 4:13-14

She came to the well in the heat of the day to escape the stares and whispers from the other women.

We don't know this woman's name, but we do know she was a Samaritan woman who had come to the well to draw water during the hottest time of day. Why would she do that? She had become an outcast with the other women. She had been tried and judged by other Samaritan women and they weren't going to let her forget it. But Jesus saw something in this woman that others refused to see, and he had plans for her.

This is one of my favorite stories among women from the Bible – well okay it runs neck and neck with Esther, and maybe Ruth and Naomi – oh well you get the picture. I think the reason this resonates with me so much is I feel a kinship with the Samaritan woman. She didn't feel worthy enough to go to the well to draw water with the other women. She believed she was lacking – she wasn't good enough to be in their company. Even though I have a feeling if Jesus had asked them for the first one without sin to cast a stone at the Samaritan woman they would have dropped their stones, turned around and left with their heads bowed in shame.

But the Samaritan woman didn't understand how much Jesus loved her, even though her train in life might have derailed a bit. She didn't even understand why he was talking to her.

The woman was surprised, for Jews refuse to have anything to do with Samaritans. She said to Jesus, "You are a Jew, and I am a Samaritan woman. Why are you asking me for a drink?"

John 4:9

I love how Jesus answered her, *"If you only knew the gift God has for you and who you are speaking to, you would ask me, and I would give you living water"* (John 4:10).

In today's language Jesus might have said, "You don't get it! I *am* the living water, and I'm offering you a drink." Jesus knew her past, as a matter of fact, he reminded her of it. Not to shame her, but to let her know that she, too, could have the living water. It was offered to everyone, no matter their past. She was so excited she dropped her jar and ran to the village to tell people about this man. "Could he be the Messiah?" She'd finally "got it." Many people were saved that day because of her. Jesus chose her to use as his vessel that day filled with living water – imperfections and all.

After my divorce, even though I didn't initiate it, I was ashamed and felt like a failure. Like the Samaritan woman, I didn't get it! I stayed away from church way too long. I had started attending Christian writer's conferences and I knew I wanted what the other women had. I returned to church, and with the help of my church family, I finally "got it!" Our worth doesn't come from our past or what we've done. Our worth comes from being a daughter of Abba. Remember, *"If you knew the gift of God and who it is that asks you for a drink, you would have asked him, and he would have given you living water."* Jesus holds that cup of living water out to us; all we have to do is accept it.

Application Questions:

Have you tasted the living water that Jesus has offered you? Does he hold your sins against you or freely offer forgiveness and redemption? In those times of doubt remember you are a daughter of the King.

_____

_____

_____

_____

_____

_____

DAY FIVE

The Samaritan Woman

Pack your bags and get ready to go on a journey to Sychar with Jesus. We are going to eavesdrop on a conversation Jesus had with the Samaritan woman at the well.

In scripture, the woman isn't named. We have no explanation as to why, but her name isn't important in this context. She is still talked about today and is a favorite of many women's bible studies. **What makes this woman so relatable? Read her story in John 4 and record what draws you to her.**

_____

_____

_____

_____

_____

Let's look at Jesus' actions on that day.

"He (Jesus) had to go through Samaria on the way. Eventually he came to the Samaritan village of Sychar, near the field that Jacob gave to his son Joseph. Jacob's well was there; and Jesus, tired from the long walk, sat wearily beside the well at noontime. Soon a Samaritan woman came to draw water, and Jesus said to her, "Please give me a drink." He was alone at the time because his disciples had gone into the village to buy some food.

John 4:4-8

Most traveling Jews would take a longer route rather than go through Samaria. But Jesus didn't do that. Jesus was a barrier breaker throughout the Bible. He touched lepers, he accepted women witnessing for him and had women followers. Take a look at the twelve men Jesus called to be his messengers to the world. Judas betrayed him, Peter denied him, Paul persecuted Christians – well you get the picture. From the beginning God and Jesus have made a point of using broken vessels to further his kingdom. In reality we are all broken. But for Jesus...

I find it interesting that when Jesus and his disciples came to the well he sent them into town for food which gave him a chance to be alone with her. **Do you think he intentionally did this so he could speak to her in private?**

_____

_____

_____

_____

The woman was shocked. She looked around and found there was no one else there – he had to be talking to her. She knew Jews went out of their way to avoid speaking to Samaritans – especially a Samaritan woman. So, she asked him, "Why are you asking me for a drink?" And this was his reply. *"If you only knew the gift God has for you and who you are speaking to, you would ask me, and I would give you living water"* (John 4:10).

There was a reason the Samaritan woman came to the well at high noon when it was the hottest part of the day. The other village women had come and gone in the coolness of the morning. She had been the latest target of the village gossipers, so she came after the other women had returned home.

She started a conversation with him about this living water. At this point she thought he was talking about real water. Like most of us in situations we don't understand, we become defensive. And that is just what she did.

"But sir, you don't have a rope or a bucket," she said, "and this well is very deep. Where would you get this living water? And besides, do you think you're greater than our ancestor Jacob, who gave us this well? How can you offer us better water than he and his sons and all his animals enjoyed?"

John 4:11-12

Why do you think the Samaritan woman became defensive at this point? Have you ever let your thoughts outrun your better judgment? Can you give an example?

_____

_____

_____

_____

_____

_____

_____

_____

But Jesus had an answer for her that would change her life and the lives of many others that day. *"Anyone who drinks this water will soon become thirsty again. But those who drink the water I give will never be thirsty again. It becomes a fresh bubbling spring within them, giving them eternal life"* (John 4:13-14).

That peaked her interest. Could this really be true? This man had water that would forever quench her thirst? She would never have to go back to the well and endure the stares and whispers from the other villagers? *"Please sir,"* the woman said, *"give me this water! Then I'll never be thirsty again, and I won't have to come here to get water."*

Then Jesus told her something that made her shudder. *"Go and get your husband."* She wondered if he knew her shame. Had he been talking to some of the villagers? No, Jews wouldn't lower themselves to talk to Samaritans. But yet, he was talking to her. This man was different!

She quickly skirted the truth. *"I don't have a husband."*

Jesus said, *"You're right. You don't have a husband – for you have had five husbands, and you're not even married to the man you are living with. You certainly spoke the truth!"*

Yikes! She didn't see that one coming. **Why do you think Jesus pointed this out to her? Did he do it in a condemning manner? Was he trying to embarrass her?**

_____

_____

_____

_____

Jesus had put the spotlight on her. Not to condemn her, but to affirm what he was about to tell her. The Samaritan woman did something that anyone in her situation might do if called out. She changed the subject. *"Why is it you Jews insist that Jerusalem is the only place of worship, while we Samaritans claim it is here at Mount Gerizim, where our ancestors worshipped?"* (John 4:19).

Jesus was ready. *"Believe me, dear woman, the time is coming when it will no longer matter whether you worship the Father on this mountain or in Jerusalem...But the time is coming – indeed it's here now – when true worshipers will worship the Father in spirit and truth. The Father is looking for those who will worship him that way..."* (John 4:21, 23).

Now she is beginning to get the picture. *"I know the Messiah is coming – the one who is called Christ. When he comes, he will explain everything to us."* She knows and believes the Messiah is coming. She was ripe for the harvest.

Then Jesus told her, *"I Am the Messiah!"*

Why do you think Jesus chose this Samaritan woman? Read verses 28-30 in John 4 and write how she reacted to this revelation.

_____

_____

_____

_____

_____

I love the way Jesus used water to teach her about the living water he had to offer. A water that would give her eternal life. She understood and wanted to share the good news with others in her village. Remember, this is a woman who came to the well at the hottest part of the day to avoid people. Now she was running toward them.

Many Samaritans from the village believed in Jesus because the woman had said, "He told me everything I ever did!" When they came out to see him, they begged him to stay in their village. So he stayed for two more days, long enough to hear his message and believe. Then they said to the woman, "Now we believe, not just because of what you told us, but because we have heard him ourselves. Now we know that he is indeed Savior of the world."

John 4:39-42

After reading about the Samaritan woman, do you think God can use you, even if you've made mistakes or sinned in the past?

_____

_____

_____

_____

_____

This is how Edith Deen summed up Jesus' encounter with the Samaritan woman.

This woman's story confirms the belief that God is no respecter of persons and that Christ came to show the inner meaning of worship. His profound teaching had quickened, enlightened, and illuminated the spirit of this worldly woman. She could now know what it meant to take of the water of life freely – not the water in the well at Sychar, near which she stood, but the spiritual refreshment which had come into her own soul after her encounter with Jesus.

My hope is after you study this chapter, you can relate to God's love for us as an ever-flowing fountain of living water.

Come and drink from that water.

CHAPTER ELEVEN

SARAH

DAY ONE

Quick! I Need Patience!

Be joyful in hope, patient in affliction, faithful in prayer.

Romans 12:12 NIV

You know what you get when you ask God for more patience? That's right. More trials to practice your patience.

We live in a world where we are used to getting what we want in minutes. Microwaves (I think I might have been the last person to get a microwave in our little town, but it didn't take me long to think 30 seconds was a lifetime), drive-through food chains, and binge watch television series without having to wait a week or two for the next episode.

Where is the excitement of waiting until the next week to see another episode of Walt Disney, Roy Rogers, or Sky King? I remember when I was in school, if we had an assignment, I had to use our Book of Knowledge encyclopedias that Grandma had bought for me and my two brothers. As I got older, I was able to go to the library and use the card index file to find what I wanted. In other words, we had to work to find the information we needed. But not today. It's at our fingertips – seconds away.

But how does that work for us when we ask God to meet a need? If I've learned one thing, it's that God's timetable is not always our timetable. In 2 Peter 3:8-9, we are told:

But you must not forget this one thing, dear friends: A day is like a thousand years to the Lord, and a thousand years is like a day. The Lord isn't really being slow about his promise, as some people think. No, he is being patient for your sake. He does not want anyone to be destroyed, but wants everyone to repent.

2 Peter 3:8-9

I think this passage is such a beautiful example of God's love for us.

But are we patient with God when we want something? We usually want it yesterday and that's not soon enough. Aren't you thankful God doesn't have our patience when it comes to waiting for us to repent? In Galatians 6:9, Paul gives some sound advice to the Christians of Galatia, *"So let's not get tired of doing what is good. At just the right time we will reap a harvest of blessing if we don't give up"* (Galatians 6:9).

Abba, I ask you to teach me to wait on you and not jump ahead and make matters worse by taking on the challenges of life by myself.

Application Questions:

Have you ever jumped ahead of God? What are some things you can do to keep you from running ahead and leaving God in the dust?

_____

_____

_____

_____

_____

_____

_____

_____

DAY TWO

See What You Did!

So Sarai said to Abram, "The Lord has prevented me from having children. Go and sleep with
my servant. Perhaps I can have children through her." And Abram agreed with Sarai's proposal.

Genesis 16:2

Sarah got just a little impatient waiting on the Lord to give her that promised baby. Even though he had already promised Abraham, *"Then the Lord said to him, "No, your servant will not be your heir, for you will have a son of your own who will be your heir"* (Genesis 15:4).

I can't fault Sarah too much, because I remember what it felt like when my friends were having babies and I hadn't been blessed with a baby yet. So, Sarah decided to help out God by offering her slave Hagar to Abraham. This was common practice during that time, when women couldn't bear their own children, the woman's hand maiden would be used as a surrogate mother. But let's dig a little deeper into Sarah's life and see how taking matters into her own hands turned out for her.

When Hagar became pregnant, at first, Sarah thought she had contrived the perfect answer without waiting on God. But right away, with the happy news, Hagar looked down on Sarah. Uh oh! Now her plan had backfired. The perfect plan became a nightmare.

And how does Sarah approach this? Does she step up and take responsibility for running ahead and leaving God behind? Well, no! Of course, not. Instead, she takes her hurt and dismay out on Abraham, even though it was her idea.

Then Sarai said to Abram, "This is all your fault! I put my servant into your arms, but now
that she's pregnant she treats me with contempt. The Lord will show who's wrong — you or me!"

Genesis 16:5 NIV

I admit I chuckled a little thinking of how similar Sarah's reactions were to women of today. One thing I have learned from studying women in the Bible is that even though their culture was foreign to us, their emotions and feelings were the very same as we experience today.

Abraham was very wise in his answer to Sarah,

"Look, she is your servant, so deal with her as you see fit." Then Sarai treated Hagar so harshly that she finally ran away.

Genesis 16:6

Abraham sounds so much like my husband. If I tell him of an event that happened to me, naturally expecting him to take my side, he very wisely utters, "Humph!"

I really shouldn't laugh at Sarah too much. Boy howdy! Have I found myself in her sandals more than once in my life – actually too many times to count. Have you ever run ahead of God and wound up making a mess of things? I know I have. Two verses come to mind when I think about how I've run ahead of God. He says, *"Be still, and know that I am God!"* (Psalm 46:10).

The other verse comes from Exodus: *"The Lord himself will fight for you. Just stay calm"* (Exodus 14:14).

Application Questions:

Can you take the time to listen for Abba's answer? The next time you become anxious and have the urge to run ahead of God, take a minute to just "be still."

_____

_____

_____

_____

_____

_____

_____

DAY THREE

I'll Wait God, but Hurry Up!

Wait for the Lord; be strong and take heart and wait for the Lord.

Psalm 27:14 NIV

Oh, my goodness! Can I relate to being impatient with God? The answer is an emphatic, "Yes!"

We say with our lips, "Here ya' go Lord. I'm laying down my burdens and worries at your feet. No, really, I mean it this time." But do our actions line up with our words? How many times do we go right back, pick up the same ole' burdens, because God didn't meet our time-table?

Waiting on God seems to be a theme that runs throughout Genesis; however, Sarah gets the blue ribbon for running the race ahead of God and leaving him in the dust. And how did that work for her? If we don't think God is working fast enough, it might lead to anxiety and panic, spurring us to move ahead without him. How do I know this? Well, let's just say, I'm sure Abba has seen my tail-lights more than once. He just shakes his head.

At times we run back to pick up that heavy load, thinking God has more important things to do, like running the world. But what does the Bible say about this?

The righteous cry out, and the Lord hears them; he delivers them from all their troubles. The Lord is close to the broken-hearted and saves those who are crushed in spirit.

Psalm 34:17-18 NIV

I can think of women we've studied who have had to wait. Sarah waited to become pregnant; Rachael waited to marry Jacob, then she waited to have a child; Esther waited on God to work a miracle to save her people; and Hannah pleaded year after year to have a child. But you know what? If we go back and look at these examples, we'll see that God heard every plea they sent to him. Did he answer them right away? No. Once again, his timing may be different than our expectations. That surely doesn't mean he isn't working in our lives even in our darkest moments. Ask Esther.

I love the way Esther chose to trust God, even though she didn't understand his ways and had no idea he had been working in her life all along. She went on pure faith. Isn't that what faith is: belief that is not based on truth? Let's take a look at how Esther approached her circumstances even when they were so dire it could mean death for her.

Then Esther sent this reply to Mordecai; "Go, gather together all the Jews who are in Susa, and fast for me. Do not eat or drink for three days, night or day. And I and my attendants will do as you do. When this is done, I will go to the king, even though it is against the law. And if I perish, I perish!"

Now, ladies, that is what I call faith. Let's all strive to be an Esther!

Application Questions:

Has God ever seen your tail-lights? What are some things you can do when that feeling, to run ahead of God, overcomes you?

DAY FOUR

Ouch, That Hurt!

But if you do what is wrong, you will be paid back for the wrong you have done. For God has no favorites.

Colossians 3:25

Consequences for our actions have been in place since the very beginning of time.

God had told Adam and Eve they could eat from any tree, but the tree in the center of the garden. What did they do? Of, course, like children do, they just had to try it out. It reminds me of the time one of my girls said a potty word, and I, being the good mother that I am, said, "Don't ever let me hear you say that again." And what did she proceed to do? I'm sure you've guessed by now. She began repeating the word over and over.

Abba's children are like that. When we are told not to do something then we push the limits as far as we can. Just to see how far we can go. And there will be many times in our lives when we will stick that toe just over the line. And that is when the consequences of our actions kick in. I'm sure you've heard the idiom, "For every action, there is a reaction."

We are all ultimately going to make mistakes that will hurt us or hurt those around us. It is a fact of life. Abba gave his children free choice, and in spite of how hard we try, we are going to mess up sometimes. Norman Vincent Peale said, "Never let any mistake cause you to stop believing in yourself. Learn from it and go on."

And don't forget how God can take our messes and give them new meaning. Sarah took matters into her own hands and the consequences were painful. Once Hagar knew she was with child she flaunted it in front of Sarah. When Sarah saw that helping God along didn't turn out the way she planned she blamed Abraham. Reminds me of the old saying, "You got yourself into this mess, you can get yourself out of it." Oh, wait, a minute; that kind of rings familiar to me.

Sarah chose to return spite for spite and began mistreating Hagar to the point she ran away. I can imagine for a few minutes Sarah breathed a sigh of relief and said to Hagar's back, "And good riddance," while shaking the dust from her hands. But God had other plans.

He takes the tattered underside of our life quilt, aka, our messes, turns the tattered side over and makes something beautiful out of it. And that is exactly what he did. An angel appeared to Hagar, and told her to return to Sarah and said, *"I will increase your descendants so much that they will be too numerous to count."*

And we know that God kept his promise to Abraham when he was a hundred years old and Sarah was ninety, and blessed them with Isaac. Abraham laughed at the notion of them having children. God had waited too long and now it wasn't possible for them to bear a child. Or was it?

Application Questions:

Sometimes I like to think of my challenges and mistakes, as walking through the fire. Have you ever made a decision that burnt your toes? We all have. Remember, even when you make mistakes, God is quick to forgive.

_____

_____

_____

_____

_____

_____

DAY FIVE

Sarah

There's a colloquialism we use all the time here in the South when we feel deeply over someone else's mistakes, "Well, bless her heart." Sounds nice, but we're really thanking God it was their mistake and not ours. That's the first thought that comes to my mind about Sarah, "Well, bless her heart." She was only trying to help God out. After all he had a lot of things to tend to and she didn't see why it would hurt to help him out just a little bit. Little did she know her decision would change the course of history.

Wait a minute. Before we delve into Sarah's story a little deeper, I have a question. Have you ever longed for something so bad that your heart ached? Did you have the urge to help God just a little bit because his timetable had not met your timetable? I have! And I wound up making things worse in the long run, instead of waiting for God's perfect timing. And that is exactly what happened to Sarah.

Let's jump right in and see what Sarah and Abraham are up to. (In Genesis 17 God changed their names Abram and Sarai to Abraham and Sarah as I will refer to them.) In Genesis 12 we begin to see what a strong woman Sarah was and how dedicated she was to Abraham and his God. God gives Abraham a directive to pick up his family and leave everything familiar to him and travel to an unknown country – talk about faith.

Let's don't rush to judgment on Sarah. Remember she also left everything she knew to go with Abraham to an unknown location. I wonder how women would react today if their husband walked into the house and said, "Pack up your things. We're moving." The wife's response being, "Moving where?" Husband's response, "I don't know. God told me to move and we're moving!" I don't know about you, but it would take a lot more convincing to get me to move under those circumstances. But not Sarah.

The Lord said to Abram, "Leave your native country, your relatives, and your father's family, and go to the land that I will show you. I will make you into a great nation. I will bless you and make you famous, and you will be a blessing to others. I will bless those who bless you and curse those who treat you with contempt. All the families on earth will be blessed through you." So Abram departed as the Lord had instructed, and Lot went with him. Abram was seventy-five years old when he left Haran. He took his wife Sarai, his nephew Lot, and all his wealth – his livestock and all the people he had taken into his household at Haran – and headed for the land of Canaan. When they arrived in Canaan, Abram traveled through the land as far as Shechem. There he set up camp beside the oak of Moreh. At that time the area was inhabited by Canaanites.

Genesis 12:1-9

Now's the time to fess up. Would you have willingly left your home and family to follow a man who didn't know where he was going? I know I'd have to think long and hard for an answer to that question. What would be your reaction if your husband came in today and said, "Pack up. We're leaving. Don't have any idea where, but we're going."

_____

_____

_____

_____

_____

_____

So Sarah made the decision to follow Abraham. Read Genesis 15.

Some time later, the Lord spoke to Abram in a vision and said to him, "Do not be afraid, Abram, for I will protect you, and your reward will be great." But Abram replied, "O Sovereign Lord, what good are all your blessings when I don't have a son? Since you've given me no children, Eliezer of Damascus, a servant in my household, will inherit all my wealth. You have given me no descendants of my own, so one of my servants will be my heir." Then the Lord said to him, "No, your servant will not be your heir, for you will have a son of your own who will be your heir." Then the Lord took Abram outside and said to him, "Look up into the sky and count the stars if you can. That's how many descendants you will have."

Genesis 15:1-5

In Genesis chapter 15 God appeared to Abraham in a vision and told him he would be protected and rewarded greatly. After reading Chapter 15 how did God promise to reward Abraham?

_____

_____

_____

_____

_____

_____

This is where the story begins to have some twists and turns thanks to Sarah's impatience. Even though God had appeared to Abraham and told him he would have his own son, Sarah scoffed at this idea. She knew she was past her childbearing years and could not grasp that God could do the impossible. So let's read on and see what Sarah has up her sleeve to help God out.

Read Genesis Chapter 16.

Now Sarai, Abram's wife, had not been able to bear children for him. But she had an Egyptian servant named Hagar. So Sarai said to Abram, "The Lord has prevented me from having children. Go and sleep with my servant. Perhaps I can have children through her." And Abram agreed with Sarai's proposal. So Sarai, Abram's wife took Hagar the Egyptian servant and gave her to Abram as a wife. (This happened ten years after Abram had settled in the land of Canaan.)

Genesis 16:1-3

What solution did Sarah come up with to make sure Abraham had a son? Was this something that would have been acceptable in their culture at that time? Considering family dynamics does this sound like a good solution? Can you guess the outcome of this decision?

_____

_____

_____

_____

_____

_____

Let's see what happened when Hagar become pregnant and gave Abraham a son, Ishmael.

> *So Abram had sexual relations with Hagar, and she became pregnant. But when Hagar knew she was pregnant, she began to treat her mistress, Sarai, with contempt. Then Sarai said to Abram, "This is all your fault! I put my servant into your arms, but now that she's pregnant she treats me with contempt. The Lord will show who's wrong – you or me!" Abram replied, "Look, she is your servant, so deal with her as you see fit." Then Sarai treated Hagar so harshly that she finally ran away.*
>
> *Genesis 16:4-6*

What in the world was Sarah thinking? How did Hagar begin to treat Sarah after she became pregnant?

_____

_____

_____

_____

_____

I can just see Hagar sticking out her tongue at Sarah saying, "Na Na Na, Boo Boo. I'm pregnant and you aren't." Or at least the equivalent to what someone might say today.

Then Sarai said to Abram, *"This is all your fault!"* This is one of my favorite lines in the story of Genesis – I actually laughed out loud as I read it, because as a woman I could relate to her reaction. And if we were all honest, most women could relate to her reaction. I've said it many times, Biblical women's cultures may have been different, but their feelings, emotions, wants, desires, and basic needs are the same as ours today. That is why we can learn so much from the women who came before us.

What was Abraham's sage advice to Sarah? What did Sarah do to retaliate against Hagar?

There have been so many times when I thought God had forgotten my desires. If my prayers weren't answered right away, then it meant it wasn't going to happen. But I know from my own experiences and the experiences from other women in the Bible that is just not true. The enemy wants us to *fix* things ourselves and not wait on God's perfect timing. We see this played out over and over in the Bible, with disastrous results. We're told in Proverbs 3:5-6, *"Trust in the Lord with all your heart; do not depend on your own understanding. Seek his will in all you do, and he will show you which path to take."*

After many years of being barren Sarah had given up hope of ever having a son. But an angel came to Abraham and said, *"I will return to you about this time next year, and your wife, Sarah, will have a son!"* Sarah, like all women, didn't want to miss a word of the conversation, so she was at the tent door listening. She knew she was well past childbearing years and laughed to herself, *"How could a worn-out old woman like me enjoy such pleasure, especially when my master – my husband – is also so old?"*

Sarah may have laughed silently, but the Lord heard her, and he didn't think it was so funny.

Then the Lord said to Abraham, "Why did Sarah laugh? Why did she say, 'Can an old woman like me have a baby?' Is anything too hard for the Lord? I will return this time next year, and Sarah will have a son."

Genesis 18:13-14

What did Sarah do when the Lord told Abraham that they would have a son? What does God say that shouts, *"Trust in the Lord with all your heart; do not depend on your own understanding. Seek his will in all you do, and he will show you which path to take"* (Proverbs 3:5)?

_____

_____

_____

_____

_____

_____

God kept his word to Sarah and Abraham, but many moons had passed since they'd first been told they would have a son. Sarah had taken matters into her own hands and changed God's plan. But he kept his promise all the same.

The Lord kept his word and did for Sarah exactly what he had promised. She became pregnant, and she gave birth to a son for Abraham in his old age. This happened at just the time God had said it would. And Abraham named their son Isaac. Eight days after Isaac was born, Abraham circumcised him as God had commanded. Abraham was 100 years old when Isaac was born. And Sarah declared, "God has brought me laughter." All who hear about this will laugh with me. Who would have said to Abraham that Sarah would nurse a baby? Yet I have given Abraham a son in his old age."

Sarah is no different than we are today, trying to rush ahead of the Lord and do his work for him instead of waiting for his timing. What God sees is the finished tapestry, what we see is the work in progress.

CHAPTER TWELVE

HANNAH

DAY ONE

It Didn't Have a Pretty Bow

Wait patiently for the Lord. Be brave and courageous. Yes, wait patiently for the Lord.

Psalm 27:14

What if, just what if, you received a long-awaited package and it was tattered, torn and wrapped up with a piece of old twine? Would your heart sink just a little? Would you question what was inside?

Life is like that much awaited package. You expected pretty gold wrapping paper with a beautiful bow on top. But what you received looked like it had been pulled from the bottom of a pile of boxes in the back of a delivery truck. Blessings can arrive in ways we never expected – and don't even know about until we look back and see, that yes, there were blessings, they just didn't come in the way or time we pictured.

I think back to the time when we had bare cupboards, living on borrowed money, and crying out to God. Why didn't he hear my plea? Was I not good enough? Was it because my faith wasn't strong enough? There were times when I honestly didn't think I was going to see fifty much less find a way out of an abusive marriage that I'd endured for over twenty years. But I did.

After I was out of the situation, I was able to look back and see where God had supplied our needs all along. During our roughest times we never went hungry, and all our needs were met. Needs not wants. And they sure didn't come in packages like I had expected. But the fact is we never went without our basic needs being met.

I have seen this same scenario played out so many times in the lives of Biblical women. And Hannah is a perfect example. Year after year she went to the temple and prayed for a son. Year after year she came home barren. I'm amazed at how faithful she was in her prayer. It's like she knew it would happen she just didn't know when.

One year while she was praying to God she cried out in anguish to the Lord, her lips moved, but no words came out. Eli the priest thought she had been dipping in the wine stock. She was so desperate she made this vow to God, *"Lord Almighty, if you will only look on your servant's misery and remember me, and not forget your servant but give her a son, then I will give him to the Lord for all the days of his life, and no razor will ever be used on his head"* (1 Samuel 1:11 NIV).

And as they say, "The rest is history." After that prayer in the temple, Hannah's whole continence changed. When she arrived at the temple she was depressed and crying – when she left, she was confident God would give her a son. Did she know exactly when? Probably not. But she was willing to wait.

Application Questions:

Are you willing to wait on God? Was there ever a time when you thought God had forgotten you, but when you reflected, realized he'd provided for your needs?

_____

_____

_____

_____

_____

_____

_____

DAY TWO

Monotony of Everyday Life

Whatever you do, work at it with all your heart, as working for the Lord not for human masters, since you know that you will receive an inheritance from the Lord as a reward. It is the Lord Christ you are serving.

Colossians 3:23-24

It's easy to brag when our faith is strong, and we've experienced God's awesomeness. But what about the quiet moments when we are alone? Do we feel the same way?

I was blessed when God brought Terri Gillespie into my life a couple of years ago. I had just started writing my devotional and I felt like I was drowning in the process. Unbeknownst to me Terri had published a wonderful devotional, *Making Eye Contact With God.* Terri is a Hebrew Christian and I have sat in awe listening to her speak of our Savior from a completely different perspective. I began to hunger for more knowledge of our forefather's faith and traditions.

I've heard Terri teach more than once specifically on finding God in quiet moments. In between journeys to the temple, Hannah had to live her everyday life. Terri wrote a short devotion on her Facebook page the other day that touched me deeply. With her permission, I'm passing it on to you.

There is that place where we give selflessly. Women who have given birth understand that moment where we must push with everything we have. But where are the ordinary moments of choosing to work from the soul?

They are the quiet moments, where no one but our Heavenly Father sees. They are the difficult moments when it would be easier to only do enough to get by. They are sacrificial moments. Small moments that seem insignificant. And large moments that seem impossible.

All of these moments make up a life dedicated to serving the Lord.

And when we have done it for the least of these, we have done it for Him.

Matthew 25:40 TLV

Whatever you do, work at it from the soul, as for the Lord and not for people.

Colossians 3:23 TLV

I have mentioned several times that my husband, Travis, and I dated for 15 years before getting married, mainly because of my responsibility of taking care of Dad and my special needs daughter, Niki. I was ecstatic so many of our friends and family, scattered around the United States, came to celebrate with us. But I remember my sister-in-law crying tears of joy. With conviction I told her, "I knew we were going to get married, I just didn't know when."

During those fifteen years life didn't stop and wait for me. Life went on. There were bills to be paid, clothes to wash, dishes to clean up, and errands to run. Too many hospital stays and doctors' appointments for Niki to even count. But I never gave up on the good things God had in store for me. And that is exactly what Hannah did year after year. Can you find your purpose in the mundane things we have to do daily while waiting on God's answers? Can you be a Hannah?

Application Questions:

Are the mundane things in life dragging you down? Do you often find yourself thinking you should be out doing the Lord's work? *"Whatever you do, work at it from the soul, as for the Lord and not for people."* **The journey you take to accomplish great things for the Lord will be filled with mundane moments. As Terri said, "Take those moments and dedicate them to God."**

_____

_____

_____

_____

_____

DAY THREE

Bloom Where You Are

I am not saying this because I am in need, for I have learned to be content whatever the circumstances. I know what it is to be in need, and I what it is to have plenty. I have learned the secret of being content in any and every situation, whether well fed or hungry, whether living in plenty or in want. I can do all things through Him who gives me strength.

Philippians 4:11-13 NIV

Okay, I have a long way to go to be content in whatever my circumstances are. But the good news is, I strive to be like Paul, *I am not saying this because I am in need, for I have learned to be content whatever the circumstances.*

We could say, "Easy for Paul to say, he's witnessed Jesus, and knows for certain the good things that are to come for him." Not necessarily. Do you know where Paul was when he penned those words? In prison. He was abused, hungry and lacking, in a prison in Rome.

2020 is a year that we all had to learn to live our best in the circumstances. In March of 2020, the Covid 19 pandemic hit the world. In all my years of living, and I'm no young chick, I had never seen anything like this before. Our whole world changed overnight. People weren't allowed to leave their houses except for necessary items and when we did, we had to wear a mask. Flights were canceled, stores closed, and we were in a world of chaos. How could I ever find contentment in this kind of life?

God slowed the world down and in doing so, forced people to stop and reconsider what was important to them. Everyday things we were used to doing suddenly stopped. Visits from family and friends, hugs and even handshakes took on a new meaning. After the initial shock of what had just taken place world-wide we were allowed to be outside for recreational purposes. I've always loved to hike in the woods, but it became even more special.

Years ago, when I first started hiking, there would be many other people enjoying the outdoors. Over the years I've seen that number dwindle and it made my heart sad. But during this awful time, parks, lakes, and recreation areas became so crowded it was hard to find a parking place. People were learning to be content in their circumstances and enjoy what they had once loved.

I saw so many things happen this past year. People began to find different ways to communicate through using the computer. People spent more time with family, turned back to God, and in general the world slowed down. Good things can come from bad circumstances

Application Question:

Are you going to be able to grow and bloom where you are? As Paul said, *"I can do all things through him who gives me strength"* (Philippians 4:13). Let's you and I, today, make the choice to bloom where we are.

_____

_____

_____

_____

_____

DAY FOUR

Broken Pots Hold More Flowers

Consider it pure joy, my brothers and sisters, whenever you face trials of many kinds, because you know that the testing of your faith produces perseverance. Let perseverance finish its work so that you may be mature and complete, not lacking anything.

James 1:2-4

Consider it pure joy when we face trials? Whoa, horse! Did I just read that right?

This is the last devotion of the last chapter in *Bloom Where You Are*. My hope is that in reading this devotional bible study companion to my book *Blooming in Broken Places* you've come to realize no matter how broken we are – God can turn our brokenness into something beautiful. We've learned about twelve broken women from the Bible who God took and used for his glory.

I don't think the above verse means that we should jump up and down enthusiastically when we are in some of our deepest, darkest moments. Nowhere in the Bible does Jesus say being his follower would be easy. As we have already studied, all his most beloved disciples faced a martyr's death except for John who was exiled and imprisoned on the Isle of Patmos.

So what lesson was James trying to convey when he wrote this to Jesus' followers? I'd like to use an illustration that might help us see just how strong and beautiful we can become through our brokenness.

Kintsugi is the art of mending broken pots with gold. This technique emphasizes rather than hides damage. Kintsugi beautifies the breakage and treats it as an important part of the object's history, and the broken pot not as something to discard, but as something more precious than it was before.

Years ago, I read a book written by Patsy Clairmont, *God Uses Cracked Pots*. I've always been drawn to books that teach us lessons through humor. And Patsy is one of the best. She took stories from her everyday life (the mundane) that might have gone a little less perfect than she expected. She then turned those short stories into lessons she had learned at the expense of her pride. And let me tell you, Patsy is a strong woman of faith, and has been sharing Jesus with many women all over the world.

I guess what I'm trying to say is Patsy took those moments that weren't so stellar and made them into something beautiful and useful just like the art of Kintsugi. We are all broken – if we weren't then Jesus wouldn't have had to die on the cross. I've heard it said, "God never wastes a hurt."

Application Questions:

Can you take your brokenness and hand it over to Abba? Can you trust him to take your broken pieces and make something beautiful? Take your broken pot and give it to God – and watch how flowers can bloom in those broken places.

_____

_____

_____

_____

_____

_____

_____

_____

DAY FIVE

Hannah

When I think of faithfulness, I think of Hannah. Barren for many years her heart ached for a child. She was married to Elkanah. But she wasn't Elkanah's only wife. As we've studied before, it was not uncommon during that time for men to marry more than one woman. Especially, if one was barren. Their lineage depended on male babies.

> In ancient times, women were primarily defined and fulfilled by their ability to have children; they didn't have careers or other ways to contribute to society or to create a sense of identity for themselves, as women do today.
>
> Despite her inability to have children, Hannah remains the love of Elkanah's life, and Peninnah is jealous. She knows that she is not numero uno in Elkanah's heart, and her jealousy drives her to ridicule Hannah. (*Women in the Bible for Dummies*)

Peninnah, Elkanah's other wife, had children. Hannah did not. Peninnah gained much pleasure from taunting Hannah. Although this was tradition for a man to have several wives it doesn't mean jealousy and friction didn't occur between the wives. We've seen this played out in many places in the Bible. **Can you list two situations from our previous bible studies where the family dynamics were very similar?**

_____

_____

_____

_____

_____

Hannah's story takes place in the first two chapters of 1 Samuel. Read 1 Samuel chapters one and two to familiarize yourself with her journey to childbirth. And it was a journey, literally and figuratively speaking. Each year Elkanah and his family would travel to the Tabernacle to worship and sacrifice to the Lord.

On the days Elkanah presented his sacrifice, he would give portions of the meat to Peninnah and each of her children. And though he loved Hannah, he would give her only one choice portion because the Lord had given her no children. So Peninnah would taunt Hannah and make fun of her because the Lord had kept her from having children. Year after year it was the same – Peninnah would taunt Hannah as they went to the Tabernacle. Each time, Hannah would be reduced to tears and would not even eat.

1 Samuel 1:4-7

What happened year after year triggering Hannah's tears? Did Hannah remain faithful to God?

_____

_____

_____

_____

There have been times in my life I was so distraught, I didn't feel like eating, and I'm fairly confident in saying you've experienced some of those devastating times in your life. Most women long for someone to talk to when their lives are challenging- someone who understands the tears. Or at the very least to comfort them. But that didn't happen for Hannah. This was a particularly hard year for Hannah and while she was fasting and crying, Elkanah, bless his heart, tried to make it better. But he was a man and was clueless to the pain she was enduring.

"Why are you crying, Hannah?" Elkanah would ask. "Why aren't you eating? Why be downhearted just because you have no children? You have me – isn't that better than having ten sons!"

1 Samuel:1:8

Whoa, what did you say Elkanah? At this point Hannah's spirit is broken. Did Elkanah make her feel better? Why not? Write about a situation where either you tried to comfort someone, or someone tried to comfort you – but the words meant to comfort just made matters worse. How could the attempt to comfort have been handled differently?

_____

_____

_____

_____

_____

_____

_____

_____

Hannah's anguish was so deep, and while she was praying, Eli the priest, was sitting and watching her. She was praying so deeply from her heart that her lips moved, but no words came out. Eli, taking this all in, jumped to conclusions and thought she had been drinking wine and was drunk. Can you image Hannah down on her knees crying out to the Lord in so much pain, crying so hard that the priest thought she was drunk?

Once after a sacrificial meal at Shiloh, Hannah got up and went to pray. Eli the priest was sitting in his customary place beside the entrance of the Tabernacle. Hannah was in deep anguish, crying bitterly as she prayed to the Lord.

1 Samuel 1:9-10

I didn't have the same issues as Hannah, but I can surely relate. When Niki was diagnosed with a brain tumor and had subsequent surgeries leaving her in a coma for four months, I felt that anguish. I remember crying out, "God, please don't let my baby die." And he didn't.

When was a time you've cried out to the Lord for answers to a desperate situation? Do you remember that feeling and does it make you better able to relate to Hannah?

_____

_____

_____

_____

_____

_____

_____

_____

Eli was so disgusted with Hannah that he told her to throw away her wine. He was indignant. How dare she come to the Tabernacle drunk! I think Hannah's reply showcases her gentle spirit. I'm not so sure I would have been as calm as Hannah was.

As she was praying to the Lord, Eli watched her. Seeing her lips moving but hearing no sound, he thought she had been drinking. "Must you come here drunk?" he demanded. "Throw away your wine!" "Oh no, sir!" she replied. "I haven't been drinking wine or anything else stronger. But I am very discouraged, and I was pouring out my heart to the Lord. Don't think I am a wicked woman! For I have been praying out of great anguish and sorrow."

1 Samuel 1:15-16

Faithfully, year after year, Hannah prayed for a son. Her faithfulness is such an inspiration to me. She believed God would answer her prayers or she wouldn't have kept praying. During the time Hannah was waiting for an answer, her heart was filled with sadness. Over and over I have experienced the incredible timing of God. But his timing isn't always our timing.

In Kirsten Mayden's article on the faithfulness of Hannah she recommends four things we can do while waiting on the Lord.

1) **Be persistent in prayer.** Let's take another look at Hannah's persistence. Year after year Hannah would call out to the Lord for a son. God calls us to persistently pray for strength, wisdom and consistency, confidence and steadfastness. We are told in Hebrews 4:16: *"So let us come boldly to the throne of our gracious God. There we will receive his mercy, and we will find grace to help us when we need it most."*

2) **Surrender your all before God.** As we continue to grow in our relationship with God and spiritual maturity, God doesn't want us to sugarcoat where we are. As we've seen Hannah sure didn't. We've studied lamenting, and we know that many of God's faithful servants had times where they poured out their hearts.

3) **Remember God's faithfulness.** During trying times, remembering God's faithfulness will strengthen, encourage and remind us that he has not abandoned us. Prayer and thankfulness for continued blessings keeps us connected and encouraged that God has not forgotten about us.

4) **Speak victory despite opposition.** Speak life and victory – walking in victory does not mean that our challenges will instantaneously disappear, but it does mean we have decided to not have them consume us. Romans 4:17 confirms this so beautifully:

As it is written: "I have made you a father of many nations." He is our father in the sight of God, in whom we believed – the God who gives life to the dead and calls into being things that were not.

Romans 4:17 NKJV

Take this time to find a verse in the Bible that matches each one of these exercises in faith that Kirsten Mayden so eloquently penned (and write them below).

_____

_____

_____

After Hannah poured out her heart to God and convinced Eli she was not drunk, he understood and blessed her. Hannah had prayed and dedicated her son to God's work if she could have a child.

And she made this vow; "O Lord of Heaven's Armies, if you will look upon my sorrow and answer my prayer and give me a son, then I will give him back to you. He will be yours for his entire lifetime and as a sign that he has been dedicated to the Lord, his hair will never be cut."

1 Samuel 1:11

"In that case," Eli said, "go in peace! May God of Israel grant the request you have asked of him." "Oh, thank you, sir!" she exclaimed. Then she went back and began to eat again, and she was no longer sad.

1 Samuel 1:17-18

Do you think Hannah praying and baring her soul before the Lord made the difference in how she felt on her way home, compared to when she arrived at the Tabernacle?

_____

_____

_____

God heard Hannah's sorrow and because of her faithful prayers, she gave birth to a son she named Samuel. She kept her promise and when Samuel was old enough, she returned him to Eli at the Tabernacle where he would serve God.

And the Lord blessed Hannah, and she conceived and gave birth to three sons and two daughters. Meanwhile, Samuel grew up in the presence of the Lord.

1 Samuel 2:21

Prayer is a powerful tool! Hannah's story is a powerful one of strength, courage, persistence and prayer, an unwavering commitment to seeking God's face.

Kirstyn Mayden

Ladies, let's make a commitment right now to take our needs boldly and consistently to God in prayer!

Printed in the USA
CPSIA information can be obtained
at www.ICGtesting.com
LVHW080110110224
771523LV00006B/793

9 781600 392429